Play Magic Golf

3rd Edition - January 2013

Prepare for a magical journey at the speed of light to steal from the world of hypnosis, meditation, Zen, NLP, universal laws, and quantum energy.

by Dr. Stephen Simpson

Dedication:

To my family Caroline, Lucy, and Ben, with thanks for our journey together. It has not always been the easiest ride, but has never been boring. We have been very lucky, and I never take this for granted.

Acknowledgements:

To my past teachers, especially those with infectious passion for their subject.

To PGA Head Professionals Roly Hitchcock and Mark Peddar for their inspired coaching, and priceless contributions in our work together.

To Dr. Karl Morris, for his inspiration.

To Chris Snape who has been exposed to tour players all of his life, and his patience in explaining to me what makes them tick.

To Dr. Simon Jenkins for his painstaking review and invaluable advice.

To Tony Wrighton for his friendship and managing my audiobooks so professionally.

To publisher Steve Emecz for his invaluable support, patience, and constant encouragement, leading to publication of the first edition.

To my clients. Without them my crazy ideas would have remained just that.

About The Author:

Dr. Stephen Simpson is a medical specialist, MBA, and Fellow of the Royal Society of Medicine. He works as an elite performance coach, and has written and presented many scientific papers at international conferences, as well as making frequent guest appearances on TV and radio. His clients include leading names from the world of sport, business, and the entertainment industries.

Dr. Simpson is also a bestselling book and audiobook author and presenter, achieving Number 1 successes in 8 countries to date; in UK, USA, Australia, Portugal, Italy, Austria, France, and Belgium. Full details of these audiobooks, books, podcasts, and videos can be found on his website.

Table of Contents

Chapter 1. Golf - What is all the fuss about   5

Chapter 2 - The pain and the pleasure   13

Chapter 3 - Unless you do something different you are guaranteed to get more of the same   23

Chapter 4 - Brain neurophysiology - take control of your emotions   32

Chapter 5 - The Zone - how to find it, how to stay there longer   36

Chapter 6 - 1st quantum law - talk tenderly - how to silence self-doubt   47

Chapter 7 - 2nd quantum law - create confidently - how to turn on the confidence tap   56

Chapter 8 - 3rd quantum Law - make movies magically - how to visualise the shot of your dreams   69

Chapter 9 - Universal energy - how to use external assistance, and not be disqualified   77

Chapter 10 - Mind over matter - how to control yourself, your golf, and your results   89

Chapter 11 - Conclusion   101

References   106

CHAPTER 1.
GOLF – WHAT IS ALL THE FUSS ABOUT?

Introduction

It is now almost exactly two and a half years since I finished writing the first edition of Play Magic Golf, and here I am writing the third edition already. Whilst I enjoy writing there are many other unfinished tasks screaming for attention. So why is this rewrite important to me? There are probably at least three reasons why this book is the most important task to accomplish today.

In a previous life I spent a short period as a university lecturer, and remember our professor reminding us that we should update at least 25% of our content every year to remain current.

At the end of the first edition of my book I listed my email address, and solicited reader comments and questions, and promised to answer each note personally. I received a huge response, and there is no doubt that this third edition will be a much better book as a result of this dialogue. I kept to my promise, and answered each note, and after a little hesitation, even the two highly critical ones. Much to my surprise I received lovely replies from both readers. That taught me a valuable lesson, and highlighted again the immense frustration that golf can inflict on so many of us, and make us behave in ways that defy logic.

I have continued to explore different mind control techniques, and how they can be adapted to make you a better golfer, and a much happier one too. Since the first edition I have also worked with many more clients, including top tour players. As usual I learnt more from them than they learnt from me, and we have enjoyed many successes during the journey. This third edition will share more details of the tools that are most likely to propel your game to the next level.

So let's crack on, and be honest about it, right from the beginning. Golf is a trivial game. Walk five miles each day for four days, hit a small white ball into a slightly larger white hole, and one inch can make the difference between winning and losing your first Major championship. Not to mention the millions of pounds, dollars and euros involved.

Who cares? Well, many people do, and some of these people have money. As we know, people with money get heard. I'm not saying that is fair, but that is the way it is, and always has been. So golf is a sport to be reckoned with.

26 million people play golf regularly. Golf has recently been appointed as an Olympic sport, and its popularity is certain to grow even further. Golfers are prepared to invest heavily in the latest equipment, and instruction, often with limited or temporary benefit. Golf instruction books sell in their millions as golfers pursue their quest for the secret. Even in the current severe recession golf has been less affected that most other sports and industries. Why should this be so?

Golf is associated with business, and in some companies is even an essential skill required to climb the corporate ladder. So love it or loathe it, golf as a sport is a force to be reckoned with. Politicians, business leaders, marketing directors, public relations experts, just to name a few examples, ignore the golfing lobby at their peril. We have already agreed that at face value golf is a triviality.

Why then are so many huge business deals sealed on the golf course? Why do intelligent men and women regularly spend five hours or more of their precious free time in the pouring rain just to hit a small ball about 85 times? Almost half of these shots will be putts, shots that a small child could perform competently.

Is there a rational explanation for the enduring and ever-growing popularity of golf? Can this attraction be explained simply as a pleasant diversion away from the stresses of modern life to beautiful countryside, an escape to the company of friends, and a return to a world with different, even old-fashioned values? Is golf even a sport, or is it an obsession, a compulsion, or even an addiction? We will come back to this question many times in search for an answer. Do these questions matter? Do these questions merit our deeper consideration?

The answer of course is 'Yes'. Thought leads to reflection, reflection leads to enlightenment, and the answers to these questions will make you a better golfer.

Golf Is More Than A Game

The reason quite simply is that finding answers to these questions will change your life. You will discover things about yourself and others that will propel you to a new level of understanding. You will have the opportunity to learn from the Illuminati of the past and the present. You will enjoy exploring the frontiers of your mind. You will achieve greater focus on what you really want, and less on what you think you want. Then you can grab it, a lot more easily than you imagined possible. How good does this sound?

I almost forgot. You will also be a better golfer, whatever that means. This is almost guaranteed.

What if you are not even a golfer? This book is for you too. I will keep the golf technical language to a minimum. The methods and tips I describe apply equally well to other sports, and to any of your other life goals too. I know this to be true because I am regularly asked to give presentations to groups of other athletes, business executives, as well as people from all other backgrounds, and see at first hand the direct results from using these tools.

I wish I could write the last chapter of this book now. It would save us both a few hours. Sadly, that is impossible. There is no way to jump from here to an explanation of the relationship between golf, life, luck, and quantum physics. It involves a journey, but I'll keep it as brief as I can. It took me more years than I care to remember to finally realise that life can be easier than I thought possible. There is a big prize waiting out there. So let us get started.

The Journey

Well, I did warn you. There is no way around it. Whatever we do in life involves a journey. That is why so many talks, films, and books narrate the author's journey. I will keep it short. A journey is a way of making sense of seemingly unconnected events, usually ending, we hope, with a powerful conclusion.

How does the word journey make you feel? Does it make you feel excited? Or does the word convey a less pleasant feeling, perhaps accompanied by uncomfortable memories? Words are powerful, they are the expression of our thoughts, and so have the power to influence our feelings. Used skilfully they can change our state of mind in seconds, often much quicker.

Perhaps then we can use words to make us feel better? Perhaps we could even use words to play better golf? Perhaps then we could control many other things too? There's a thought! We will talk much more about this later.

A journey is a process of development. A gradual passing from one situation to another situation that is regarded as more advanced. A metaphor is a figure of speech applied to something that is not literally applicable. Its derivation from Latin means to carry over, and from Greek to transfer.

'Journey' and 'metaphor' are two distinct words, and yet much closer in meaning in their derivations. Before the age of TV, radio, and books the most entertaining storytellers and jongleurs knew the importance of the skilful use of metaphors to make their point. I will do my best to do the same. To convey complex ideas in a simple form that you can use immediately. I will also do my best to be entertaining, and share just a bit of my background with you.

I am a medical doctor. The only two subjects that interested me at medical school were the unlikely combination of surgery and psychiatry. Not surprisingly I scored high marks in these subjects, but struggled in most of the others, especially in the subjects that required hours of parrot-like memorisation. I did not have that kind of brain.

It is only recently that I have recognised that I did, and still do have a variety of attention deficit disorder. I dislike these labels because they are by nature only approximations, but they are the best we have at the moment, as long as they are not taken too literally, or used as criticism.

I have no problem focusing my concentration on things that interest me, but have great difficulty marshalling the will power to address other issues that bore me, or have no obvious relevance. I have also since discovered that there a lot easier ways to learn stuff than the way I was taught, and these are the methods I will use in this book.

I have always loved travel. Three years after graduation I decided to work in Africa for a year. Little did I know then how much this would change my life. The following years were a blur. I worked in war-torn Angola for seven years, the deserts of Oman, the swamps of Nigeria, and the steppes of Kazakhstan, and visited many other countries on business too.

During this time I was mugged, imprisoned briefly several times (usually in the Democratic Republic of Congo), shot at, mortared, and almost killed in a helicopter incident. In other words at the time I thought I was having fun, and in retrospect was lucky to survive these exploits with barely a scratch.

I also enjoyed fighting against esoteric tropical diseases, such as Marburg. This is a variety of Ebola, and just about the deadliest disease on the planet. I was part of the team that responded to the World's largest ever outbreak of Marburg, in Angola. This was not an experience I would have chosen, but learnt a lot from it. You do not learn how people react in a crisis from the comfort of a plush office.

I would have preferred not to have experienced near-fatal malaria, but the associated out-of-body experience was interesting, in a detached way. I could also have done without the less serious dengue, dysentery, and the dubious delights of Tumbu infection. It is not much fun incubating and then hatching maggots under your skin.

Despite these challenges, or perhaps even because of them I loved my work and the spirit of adventure. I loved being a hands-on doctor and a coach in a challenging environment. I valued the friendship of the tight-knit and tough expatriate community. I similarly valued the friendship of the local people, who were far more forgiving of my cultural naivety than I deserved.

What did I learn that will make you a better golfer? I learnt about magic. I saw at first hand the Wasim fire healers, the witch doctors, and the shamans maim and kill my patients, despite my protestations. I was bewildered and could not understand why my patients often chose to consult their traditional healers first, and use me only when all else failed.

Curiously on rare occasions I also saw the healers achieve results that were far beyond what was possible with my modern medicines. I wanted to find out how they did this, and it took me a long time to even begin to understand.

The healers achieved their results by magic. Magic is a special, mysterious, or inexplicable quality, talent, or skill[1]. I will use this word many times, with this definition in mind. I doubt we will ever be able to fully explain any of these inexplicable events, although science is beginning to offer some pointers. We are beginning to see some indistinct shadows through the veil of mystery. That is more than enough for now. Almost certainly there are many scientific explanations waiting to be discovered. For the moment though the shadows are all we have.

All that is necessary to share this journey is that you can accept that some things in life are beyond rational explanation. Then you are near-certain to become a better golfer. You will also be able to carry these benefits over to your life outside golf, as many readers have recounted in their wonderful letters. If you so choose.

People do not change their personalities when they step onto a golf course. The same knowledge, attitudes, skills, and personal beliefs are carried from the locker room to the course. Those people, people like you and me, are the same people on the golf course as they are at work, as they are at home with their families, and as they are as they lie in bed with their dreams. They are all capable of using magic.

The key to being a magic golfer is to give room in your busy life for your largely untapped talent to thrive. It will require some thought on your part. At the end of each chapter you will find a Meditation Booth. Briefly review the chapter, your scribbled notes, and your highlighted text.

Identify three points that you believe can help you immediately or at least in the very near future. Write them down in the Booth.

Then close your eyes for just a few minutes, and think of nothing. Not many people can do this, so it is perfectly acceptable to just drift away with some other pleasing thoughts. Perhaps they might be great shots you have played, or wonderful courses you have visited, whatever. It is your choice.

At some point during or after your meditation, all at a rate and speed that is appropriate, you will experience an epiphany moment. The light bulb will illuminate. Write it down before you forget it. Then you are truly Master of your game, a rare commodity in the world of golf.

During the following pages our journey will take us at the speed of light through classical philosophy, modern philosophy, psychology, NLP, Zen, hypnosis, meditation, Universal Laws, Natural Energy, Quantum Physics, and many other things too.

Some readers have read the whole book in one sitting. There are no rules, but generally I would recommend just reading a chapter or two at each sitting. An exception is a lady who started reading at midnight, and finished at 3AM. She was a County player, and wanted to call me then, but considerately resisted the temptation. Parts of the book reminded her of her deceased father, and how he had taught her to play golf, and inspired her with his passion. She cried during some sections, but also felt a sense of release. Despite being in her sixties she achieved one of her best scores the following day.

Another reason that I tell these stories, and they are all true, is that they can inspire you. Your mind knows that if these methods work for others, then they can work for you too.

Meditation Booth

Three Nuggets For Now
1.

2.

3.

CHAPTER 2.
THE PAIN AND THE PLEASURE

I have a childlike fascination with paradox, and golf is certainly paradoxical. On the one hand is the pain associated with golf. I play with golfers regularly, and listen to their stories in the bar afterwards. The moments of joy are usually heavily outnumbered by the groans of despair. I can accurately estimate the financial cost of their sport. I can only guess at the time spent away from families and work, and what cost or benefit this might carry.

On the other hand I am still puzzled by the nature of the elusive reward that motivates golfers to endure the pain of the poor scores, the slow rounds, and (sometimes) the dreadful weather.

Part of the reward, or hook, is obvious. There are many happy times of personal satisfaction, healthy exercise, or even a big prize. We are social animals, and so the shared fun, laughs, and banter are also a huge part of the enduring attraction of golf in the raw. However, this still does not take me very much closer to finding the answer to the question. Is golf a sport, or is it an obsession, a compulsion, or even an addiction?

I'll leave this question hanging a little longer. I am sure the next question will be of far more immediate importance to you.

Is it possible to have a lot more fun playing golf, a lot less frustration, and shoot lower scores too?

Unequivocally 'Yes!' It is a lot easier than you might think. It comes as a huge surprise to the golfers I've worked with in one way or the other. Here are four more questions that we will find answers to in the following pages.

Does this mean you will shoot a magical score every day? Certainly not – you have no control over bounce, whether a putt drops or just lips out, and how other players score.

Will my system give you the best possible chance of controlling your emotions and finding 'The Zone', and so playing to the best of your ability on the day? Certainly.

When you walk off the 18th green can you be satisfied that you have done your best, and can feel proud of your efforts, irrespective of your score, rather than beating yourself up? Certainly. Perhaps you might even have a smile on your face!

Intriguingly can you believe that players who stay in the present and follow the process, have no need to worry about scores or results?

Addressing Envelopes Can Be Fun

Eventually most people hitch up with a spouse or partner. It's in our genes, part of the programming that that has helped make Homo sapiens the dominant species on our Planet, at the moment.

Later still come children to many of us. Logically this is crazy. We give up freedom, time and money for others.

Fortunately life and golf are not logical. There are paybacks. My family and friends are forgiving, and generous with their time and love. They pretend to enjoy being guinea pigs, and sharing my bizarre psychological experiments.

Bizarre maybe, but to the surprise of many, my initial experiments were phenomenally successful. Rapid cuts in handicaps were followed by competitions won, and even multiple holes-in-one. My first client was my wife Caroline. She had been stuck with a handicap of 27 for many years, and now plays off 13. She had never had a hole-in-one. Within a six month period she collected three, and two of them were in major club competitions. She has just added a fourth, also in a competition. Was this a coincidence? Of course it was. However in a later chapter we will ponder whether our universe is as random as we might believe.

As with all therapy though, there were also unexpected side-effects. My clients and more often their partners – marital or playing – noticed something rather curious. My golfers were happier, calmer, and more confident. Not only on the golf course, either.

I worked with more people. I soon realised four hour sessions were too long for both of us. I cut our sessions to one hour. Then I worried I was pushing out too much information in too short a time. I worried I might forget to include key parts of my method. I recorded in my study a 30 minute CD to give to my clients to take away, more for my peace of mind than theirs. I listened to it, and it sounded awful.

I booked a studio and an engineer, hoping for a more professional recording. I had no idea what this would involve, but again I got lucky. Engineer Mark held my hand, introduced me in a gentle way to the delights of sticky mouth, gasping, page turn rustle, drop ins, bouncedowns, and many other dark mysteries of the recording craft. Two hours later I emerged into the sunlight as a professional recording artist with a Master CD in my sweaty palm.

I gave my CD to friends. Mostly they liked it, or at least that is what they told me. Copies were passed around, and I started to receive more objective feedback from people I had never met. A typical response was,

'I've never heard the end of your recording, I always drop off to sleep.'

Well, as a self-deluded devotee of positive thinking I chose to take this as a compliment. I ran out of friends and family very quickly. Not much later I'd exhausted the friends of friends too. It was time for another social experiment.

I decided to sell my CD on eBay. Could my CD help a complete stranger play better golf? Cautious confidence was soon replaced with doubt. I suspect any artist offers their work to the Universe with trepidation. I certainly did.

eBay is a ruthless marketplace, as you may know from your own experiences. If you are lucky enough to sell your product the problems might just be starting. I sold one CD in the first month. The eBay process is standard. The buyer receives my CD, listens to it, and then writes their feedback, good or bad. This is public, for the World to share.

After my first sale coincidentally I listened to a programme on BBC Radio 4 about singer/songwriter Vashti Bunyan. Vashti recorded her debut album in 1970 with little initial success. After she read the first critical review of her first solo album she was so upset she never read another review, and never recorded anything else until 30 years later. She went walk-about for many years, and so was unaware that her album was slowly achieving cult status. Happily for her, and her loyal fans she did record a second album, 30 years later.

I could understand in a small way how she felt. I suspect my horse and cart days are behind me, but I am certain that if my first review had been critical that would have very likely signalled the end of the first tentative steps of my recording career.

On the 28th August, 2008 the following buyer comment was posted.

'Excellent ebayer, delivery next day as promised.'

Wow, I'll take this as positive!

Three more sales followed in September, and four in October. In less than a year my CD sold more copies than any other in the admittedly small market of golf hypnosis. I doubt it was the best, but for some reason people liked it. All the reviews were positive, and the only criticism was,

'CD was as described although presentation box minimal.'

The experiment had succeeded, and even exceeded my expectations. I had even covered the cost of making the CD, which was an unexpected bonus. What was more important was that I now had a network of 'Magic Golfers'. Their feedback was priceless to me. We swopped notes from all around the World, and still do. Now I have many more members who sign up for my free monthly newsletter. I loved their awesome success stories, and was shocked by some of their tribulations. I could not believe it but some had been driven close to suicide by their frustrations with this trivial game. I was humbled that I had been able to help them in some way.

I was also surprised by how many clients had used my methods in other areas of their lives. I was honoured that one with a phobia of public speaking, much to his surprise and delight, had been able to make the speech at his daughter's wedding, and even enjoyed it.

I knew I could not stop now. I recorded more CDs, and not just golf titles. The digital market was changing fast. More people now bought audiobooks, and less bought CDs. Now the CD market is dead, at least for my products, but the growing trend continues to be for audiobooks, and more recently for videos, especially on YouTube.

I was fortunate to be granted a publishing contract for my audiobooks, and so was in the right place at the right time. I was lucky, and we will consider the nature of luck in a later chapter. For the moment suffice it to say that many people believe that they create their own luck, at least to some extent.

The goddess of luck was certainly smiling on me. Zen Hypnosis: Confidence was the bestseller in any category for most of the first half of 2010 in UK on iTunes. All the titles charted in the major international outlets, and reached Number 1 in Australia, USA, France, Austria, Italy, Belgium and Portugal too.

I remained grounded, and knew my audiobook was not the best on sale, probably by a long way. But I also knew that for one reason or another it sold more copies than any other. Something about it resonated with people. Was it the title, the artwork, or for want of a better word, was I just lucky?

There was something missing though. The people who buy my audiobooks on iTunes are largely anonymous. I miss the emails, the stories, and the feedback that all coaches require to calibrate their methods. Curiously I also miss addressing envelopes, writing little notes to strangers, and posting CDs.

There is a point to this story. My first naïve faltering steps to record a CD to give to my clients for free had metamorphosed into a Number 1 best-selling audiobook. It had developed a life of its own, and its success was responsible for 14 other titles, tthree books, countless presentations, studio guest invites, and many videos too. Now follows my first golf tip to you.

'About time too' I hear you say.

If you can handle this tip you can handle anything. You probably will not need to read any further. However, I know that this issue is one of the hardest challenges in life to overcome. In one way or another, this tip is what the rest of this book will address in many different practical ways. Here we go.

Focus on the process and the results will take care of themselves.

In other words do the best job you can at the time, imperfect as that might be, and do not worry where it might all end. You might be surprised. You might get a lot more than you expected. As I did when I recorded my first CD in my study

Another way to describe this state of mind is to just stay in the present. An increasingly popular word for this at the moment is mindfulness. We will talk much more about this later, and how you can learn how to stay in the present, cocooned in the sanctuary of process.

What Goes Around Comes Around

As I researched reference sources for this book I became increasingly aware that very little in life is new. So it is with golf too.

Whilst this might be disappointing to those searching for novelty I suspect it will be reassuring for many others. Tried and trusted methods have proven their worth time after time over the centuries. The content of these messages is consistent, and only the packaging has changed.

Last year I published my second book, Push at Open Doors. It is a personal development title, and does not mention golf, although its messages definitely would benefit any golfer. Briefly the book is about how to develop mindfulness, and then how to use it for greater success, health, wealth, and happiness.

The previous comments about very little in life being new applied even more forcefully to this book. We are surrounded by truth, but remain largely unaware of it. So my job is to gently suggest some of these universal truths. Then you will be able to save yourself much time. You will have a lot more fun too. My role has been to select the methods that have proven to be most helpful for clients. I also hope to explain them in an engaging and relevant manner for the modern golfer.

I have always been fascinated by the human mind, and how some people have been able to reach the pinnacle of human achievement. They have scaled these heights by using their brain in different and more skilful ways than the rest of us mere mortals. I wanted to know how they do it.

I did not have time to work this out for myself, even if I could. From the outset I sought out the best personal development gurus I could find. People like Dr. Richard Bandler, the co-founder of NLP; Dr. Paul McKenna, world famous hypnotist, author, and personal development guru; expert communicator John La Valle; and Michael Neill, internationally renowned success coach and best-selling author. I trained with them, and learning from the best is always the wisest investment a person can make.

More recently I trained with Dr. Karl Morris, one of the best, if not the best, mind coaches in the world of golf. When somebody has worked successfully with Graeme McDowell, Darren Clarke, Lee Westwood, Louis Oosthuizen, and Paul McGinley, you would be very foolish not to listen to them very carefully indeed.

I also sought out views from the Illuminati of the past. I read selectively from deep thinkers like Freud, Jung, and others. A pattern started to emerge. I dug deeper and older.

I explored the works of Plato, Aristotle, Socrates, and even my medical colleague Hippocrates. The pattern became even clearer.

Nothing is new. Despite their obvious differences these brilliant men and women are all saying much the same thing. Their uniqueness comes from the way they use these Universal truths.

My role by comparison has been extremely minor. It has been to unsheathe my rusty scalpel and clumsily hack away a few nuggets that appear to shine the brightest.

- Use these nuggets for your psychology Ph.D. thesis and you will fail.
- Use these nuggets on the golf course and you are almost guaranteed to be a better golfer.
- Use these nuggets off the golf course and you will be truly rich.

How To Use This Book

It is almost certain that your golf will improve immediately as a result of reading Play Magic Golf. A huge amount of information will be pushed in your direction. Some of it will aid conscious thought; much more will develop the largely untapped power of your unconscious mind.

Clients frequently worry that they will forget some of this important information. That is not likely, because my system is simple, and the brain remembers everything. It just needs a bit of help with its filing system.

However, just as it is almost certain that your golf will start to improve immediately as a result of reading this book, it is equally almost certain that unless you remind yourself periodically of the key insights you discovered then over time these huge improvements will erode. The pendulum will always revert to its balance point if you allow it too. Your challenge is to find a balance point for a much larger pendulum.

This is the main value of what is to follow. Refer to it from time to time. Play Magic Golf is not a text book to put on the shelf and forget. It is a living testament to your progress as a golfer, and maybe as a person too.

Scribble in the margins to your heart's content, just as you liked to do when at school. However this time I promise you that you will not have your knuckles wrapped.

You may choose to use highlighter pens. If so, choose your colours with care. Red means Danger, right? It's probably best to reserve red for the bits that you know instinctively will not help you.

Use your favourite colour for the bits that most strongly resonate with you. I know from working with clients that some of these nuggets are the ones that will catapult you to the next level.

Use a neutral colour for the stuff you are not sure about. In time you'll ditch some of this with your red pen. Other bits will turn to your favourite colour in front of your eyes. Whatever is left may take at least one lifetime to digest.

Writing Is The Doing Part Of Thinking

When I see a new client for the first time I ask for only two things. I ask that my client has an open mind. There is no problem with scepticism, I can handle that.

The second requirement is a brief note from them detailing the issue. The note is vital to me because at a superficial level it will describe the client's view of their problem, and their desired outcome. My performance will be measured against this yardstick.

At a deeper level something magical often happens when my client writes their note to me. Their note develops its own life too. I start to appreciate the words they use, I gain a glimpse of their view of the world, and what makes them tick. I start to develop the skeletons of strategies that I believe they will find helpful.

Their notes are often anything but brief. The magic often hides in the final paragraph.

'Steve, I'm sorry I rambled on a bit. I hadn't thought of some of these things for years. You will be really surprised, but I actually feel a lot better already just for writing this down.'

As you can guess I am not in the least surprised. I expected it. So I'd like to share another fundamental point with you right now.

Writing is the doing part of thinking.

Writing is a simple way to connect to the unconscious mind. We call this a flow state, not unlike the zone in golf.

I'll put it another way.

• Good intentioned thoughts often remain as good intentioned thoughts.

• Spoken thoughts sometimes get done.

• Written thoughts often lead to unimagined success.

Meditation Booth

Three Nuggets For Now

1.

2.

3.

CHAPTER 3.
UNLESS YOU DO SOMETHING DIFFERENT YOU ARE GUARANTEED TO GET MORE OF THE SAME

The chances are that you love golf, and all the stories and characters that make golf such an entrancing and yet frustrating game. You have almost certainly invested much time, money, and effort in buying the clubs, clothes, shoes, membership, and lessons, and lots more besides. One day you can play out of your skin, and the next day shoot one of your worst rounds ever.

Where is the logic in that? Well, I have news for you – there isn't any logic in golf. We have to find a different part of our brain to provide answers to these questions, of which much more later.....

Now let us start with a fundamental Truth. You will only move to the next level in golf when you do something different; otherwise, you are guaranteed to get more of the same.

Whilst lessons, books, and coaching CDs all have their value, the greatest investment in time and money you can make is to develop the mental side of your game. When you follow my proven system The 3 Quantum Laws Of Golf you are almost guaranteed to become a better golfer, and enjoy more happiness both on and off the Golf Course.

The value of a system is that it provides a foundation that is easy to remember. There are only three components of my system; words, confidence, and visualisation. Almost everything in this book will fall into one of these categories.

I make almost no reference to technical skills; that is not because they are not important, it is because they are not that important. Most golfers overvalue technical issues, and greatly undervalue their most valuable resource – their brain.

The reason that small technical corrections often work in the short term is that they give you confidence. Get rid of the old and bring on the new. However once the novelty has worn off, then so too do the benefits. That is why it makes a lot more sense to discover natural ways to capture this confident feeling. These methods work not just in the short term, but for months and years.

Swing Fundamentals – Golf Is An Easy Game, Isn't It?

Of course it is easy. I said so right at the beginning. All you have to do is to just hit a small white ball into the hole. Walk five miles each day for four days and one inch can make the difference between winning and losing your first Major championship.

Just take one shot at a time. Remember the importance of wind, slope, stance, grip, balance, weight transfer, swing arc, wrist action, shoulder turn, leg action, head position, and so I could go on. Don't worry. You have plenty of time to work this out – about one second. Perhaps it is not so simple after all. Now we are beginning to understand the problem.

Teaching professionals claim that if you practise hard, and have regular lessons you may reduce your handicap by two or more shots per season. I am sure this is possible, but judging by the clients who come to see me this does not happen to everyone. More commonly golfers become confused, tense, and very frustrated. They are trying to think of so many things at once that they are suffering from analysis paralysis.

Sports such as football, tennis, and cricket are very fast-moving, with little time to think. The best players have superb hand-eye coordination, and razor-sharp reflexes. However golf is a very different game, and presents its own unique challenges. A round of golf can now take upwards of five hours to complete, and so there is plenty of time for thinking.

This is often when the damage is done. The brain takes over, leading to too much analysis, and introspection. All too often this is where the negative thoughts creep in. It seems that the bad shots are the ones that are remembered, and harsh self-criticism is often the norm. Fortunately there is a much better way to play and think about golf.

Skilful Objectives

If we do not know where we are going then any road will take us there. In other words whatever we do in life is it is very important to have a goal. The skill lies in choosing the correct goal.

We should all have one overarching goal in life. This is something that is so important to us that we want to be reminded of it all the time. It helps to build a self-fulfilling prophecy, and this important subject will shortly be discussed in more detail.

For the professional tournament golfer an example would be winning a Major championship. The more different ways you can remind yourself of your goal each day the more successful you are likely to be. There are many ways to do this. Examples include writing the goal on stickers and fixing them to the bathroom mirror, the refrigerator, using the goal as a screensaver on your computer, mobile phone, and alarm clock. The more places you can think of the more likely you are to reach that goal.

Olympic swimming champion Michael Phelps is a great example of the importance of constant reminders. When he announced his goal of 8 gold medals in China he was incensed by an article expressing doubts that he could deliver this prediction. He pinned this article to his locker and stared at it every morning until he left for China. Was this visualisation? Was it a powerful affirmation? Or was it a self-fulfilling prophecy? Who knows, but the important thing is that it worked for him.

'People say that I have great talent, but in my opinion excellence has nothing to do with talent. It is about what you choose to believe and how determined you are to get there. The mind is more powerful than anything else[2].'

The problem often lies in choosing subsidiary goals in our everyday life. You have decided to invest time and money to buy and read Play Magic Golf. What do you expect to gain from this investment? Is it to win a club competition, to reduce your handicap, to improve your consistency, to gain confidence, or just to have more fun? Perhaps all of these are your objectives?

I always ask clients to share their goals with me. It tells me a lot about them, and helps to develop their success strategies. Many clients want more confidence, more money, a new relationship, a new house, or a new car. I would like to think that I can help them achieve these goals. My worry is whether this will make them happy?

I have spent most of my life living and working in the developing world. I have seen many happy people who have little more than the shirt on their back. I have also seen others who have just about everything they could possibly desire, and were not happy. This has led me to the conclusion that some objectives in life are helpful and others are unhelpful. Often the way we think about an objective can make all the difference.

Generally if an objective can be carried in a huge wheelbarrow it is likely to be unhelpful. In other words most material possessions fall into this category. There is nothing wrong with material possessions. However they should not be a goal in themselves, but rather a result of doing other things to the best of your ability. Many helpful objectives are more difficult to quantify and define. To have more confidence, more love, more courage, more happiness, or more personal satisfaction, are all examples of helpful objectives.

For most of our lives at school, at work, and at home we have been conditioned to recognise success in terms of material possessions. Society sadly places less value on some of the qualities that I have listed above. Certainly in golf, and in just about all other areas of their lives too, I advise clients not to focus just on results. Far more important is focusing on process.

In other words if we stay in the present and do the best job we can at that moment we do not need to worry about the results of our efforts. They will take care of themselves. There are countless examples to support this statement. Many mountaineers describe a sensation of anticlimax after climbing a particularly difficult mountain. They remember with much more lasting satisfaction the journey that took them there. Business executives remember with pleasure the earlier years of their career, whilst lottery winners have all the money they have ever dreamt of, but are not always content.

So it is with golf. Stay in the present, enjoy every shot, and the results usually take care of themselves.

Left/Right Brain Quiz

Please spend a minute or two completing this simple Quiz. Choose the option in each column that most applies to you. Some of the choices are tricky. Usually your first thought is your best thought. Just like golf.

When you have finished the quiz count the ticks in the Right Brain column. Your overall score is not important, but it does reveal some basic elements of your unique personality.

LEFT BRAIN	RIGHT BRAIN
Practical	Impulsive
Likes detail	Likes general outline
Prefers safety	Prefers to take chances
Loves language	Love symbols

LEFT BRAIN	RIGHT BRAIN
Facts count	Dreams count
Live in the past	Live in the future
Logical	Emotional
Prefers science	Prefers philosophy
Develop plans	Develop options
Understand	Imagine
Identify item by name	Identify item by function
Prefers landscape art	Prefers abstract art
Loves documentaries	Loves fantasy movies

If you have scored between 5-9 points you have an almost equal balance, and can probably flit to and from left and right brain scores depending on what you are doing, and your mood.

Score between 0-6 points and you have Left Brain dominance. I can often make a fair guess at a client's occupation from their scores. Left brain dominance careers would include medicine, law, finance, critic, audit, and analyst.

Right brain dominance with scores of 10-13 suggests occupations that include music, art, public relations, marketing, and politics. Curiously many of the best golfers that I work with fall in this category.

I stress that whilst your individual score is interesting, it is of minor importance. What is far more important is the change in your score as you start to think differently about some things, and develop your mental powers accordingly. Even a small shift from left to right brain balance can make a huge difference to your golf, and the enjoyment that ensues.

Left Brain/Right Brain Model. Use Your Right Brain To Play Magic Golf

This model is only a model. There is no anatomical border in the brain that divides left and right brain functions. Other psychology models also highlight a similar bipolarity of thought, such as those that differentiate between the Conscious and Unconscious Mind.

Ideally the two parts of our mind share a common agenda, and coexist in perfect balance and harmony. Sadly often they do not, and therein hide possible clues to some of the answers.

Dr. Bob Rotella talks about the power of subconscious thought in his excellent book Your 15th Club[3]. Another imaginative example directly related to golf is the basis of Galway's Inner Game of Golf [4] book, where he describes the different characters of Self 1 and Self 2.

I choose to use the left/right brain model because, like many others, I found the following example so compelling. This is an extract from the product description of the wonderful book My Stroke of Insight[5].

'On the morning of the 10th December 1996, Jill Bolte Taylor, a thirty-seven-year-old Harvard-trained brain scientist experienced a massive stroke when a blood vessel exploded in the left side of her brain.

A neuroanatomist by profession, she observed her own mind completely deteriorate to the point that she lost the ability to walk, talk, read, write, or recall any of her life, all within the space of four hours. As the damaged left side of her brain – the rational, logical, detail and time-oriented side – swung in an out of function, Taylor alternated between two distinct and opposite realities: the euphoric Nirvana of the intuitive and emotional right brain, in which she felt a sense of complete well-being and peace; and the logical left brain, that realized Jill was having a stroke and enabled her to seek help before she was lost completely.'

The left brain is described as the logical and analytical Centre of conscious thought. In today's hectic environment this part of our brain is preoccupied with diaries, task lists, and planning all our activities. It is so busy that it often overwhelms the more creative and deeper functions of the right brain. Left brain people love logic, facts, and are very detail oriented. They are often strong in mathematics and science. Their lives are practical, and the present and the past are very important to them.

The right brain is where unconscious deeper thoughts and memory are stored. People often describe having a gut feeling that a certain course of action was the right thing to do; they will talk about following their instincts, premonitions and hunches.

The Right Brain is the part of the brain where golfers get in the zone. The zone is the magical place where everything is easy, where the outside world is for once a little muted, and where we feel very relaxed and confident. Most of us have experienced this at some time in our lives, but have difficulty recreating this feeling at will.

Right brain people claim to be more in tune with their feelings; they have vivid imaginations, and love fantasy. The present and the future are more important to them than the past. On occasions, they tend towards being impetuous and delight in taking risks.

The right brain is the home of great golf, and I will refer to it many times. It will take a change in the way you think about golf, and your life outside golf, to learn how to use your right brain more than you do now. The right brain is where language, hypnosis and meditation work their magic. I will talk more about these fascinating and often misunderstood subjects in the next chapter.

Meditation Booth

Three Nuggets For Now
1.

2.

3.

CHAPTER 4.
BRAIN NEUROPHYSIOLOGY –
TAKE CONTROL OF YOUR
EMOTIONS

What Goes On In Your Head Comes Out In Your Life

Too often our thoughts become a self-fulfilling prophecy, and Henry Ford knew the power of such thoughts.

'Whether you think you can or think you can't - you are right.'

Clearly it is going to make for a much easier round of golf if we think we can, rather than that we cannot. It is possible to direct your thoughts in this direction, but does require some practice.

Author and social scientist Ralph Waldo Trine found that the best way to control his emotions was by adopting an active rather than passive outlook on his life.

'To get up each morning with the resolve to be happy... is to set our own conditions   to the events of each day. To do this is to condition circumstances instead of being conditioned by them.'

This does not sound too difficult, but to be able to have this resolve every day might be more problematic? This is the crux, and applies to all self development. It involves change. Anybody can change almost any behaviour for a single day, but to make a permanent change requires commitment and making choices. It is not as difficult as it might sound, and there are useful tools to help.

Before we examine some of the ways that will help you exert greater control over your emotions it will be helpful to know a little more about how your brain works.

The truth is that the brain remains one of the last barriers to scientists. Neurophysiologists have barely begun to unravel the secrets. What we know is that we use but a fraction of our brain's potential. There are some parts of our brain that are rusty, or that we have forgotten how to use. As with any part of our body and mind we use it or lose it.

Emotions and gut-feelings are possibly shortcuts that the brain uses to process huge amounts of information and thus influence behaviour. If this is true then such short cuts are vital to golf. There is so much information to process when evaluating how to hit a golf ball with infinitesimal precision. Without such shortcuts the sport would be impossible.

How good you feel (or not) before you hit your shot is not surprisingly a strong predictor of the result. You will have experienced this yourself many times. No doubt there is a sense of frustration as you struggle to recreate this feeling of confidence over the ball.

By recognising this feeling for what it is, whether good or bad, will be a major step forward in your golfing progress. You have discovered a key to unlock the golfer inside you. Now you just need a bit more help to pick the lock.

In other words there are tools that you can use to control your emotions. You are not a passenger in your body. When you master these tools you master your emotions. You feel better inside yourself, and curiously you play magic golf.

How you feel at any given moment depends on chemicals. Through the ages many have discovered the mind-altering properties of alcohol, cannabis, LSD, and legions of other external chemicals. Fewer have discovered the much more valuable and helpful secret that the body, especially the brain, manufactures its own chemicals that control your emotions.

These chemicals include neurotransmitters such as serotonin, dopamine, and noradrenaline. They are usually manufactured with perfect purity, and interact with each other in exquisite balance. This is just one of the many miracles in your body of which you are totally unaware.

The science behind all this is staggeringly complex. Medicines have already been developed by brilliant scientists to treat conditions such as anxiety, depression, attention deficit disorders, Parkinson's disease, and schizophrenia. More medicines are discovered every year, and no doubt more Nobel prizes will be awarded in this area too.

I am going to share with you some techniques that will empower you to gain greater control over your emotions. You are unlikely to become an advanced yogi (practitioner of yoga). These are people who can control to an extraordinary degree functions that are thought to beyond conscious control, such as pulse, breathing rate, emotional state, and pain.

Fortunately you do not need to. You only require a small shift in your right brain balance to play great golf. So too do you only need to gain a little more control of your emotions to unlock much more of your latent golfing power.

These are some of the unhelpful emotions my clients have associated with their golf, often for many years. I wonder how many have applied to you in the past, or perhaps even now? How many can you identify in your playing partners?

- Anger
- Annoyance
- Anxiety
- Depression
- Despair
- Disappointment
- Embarrassment
- Fear
- Frustration
- Loathing
- Misery
- Rage

- Shame
- Suffering

Some of these are very strong and destructive emotions to attach to a simple game of golf. Do you remember me asking whether golf is a sport, or is it an obsession, a compulsion, or even an addiction?

Nobody other than ourselves forces us out on to the golf course, so there are clearly powerful internal influences at work. These are some of the more helpful emotions I have helped my clients rediscover. They are far more pleasurable.

- Curiosity
- Ecstasy
- Euphoria
- Happiness
- Hope
- Joy
- Pride
- Surprise
- Wonder

Of these I consider happiness to be the most important. Happy golfers shoot lower scores than unhappy ones. They also have a lot more friends. Like all things in life happiness has to be worked at. A little more happiness leads to much lower scores. In the next chapter I will share with you some secrets of happiness, and how they can lead you to the natural and elusive home of great golf – The Zone.

Meditation Booth

Three Nuggets For Now
1.

2.

3.

CHAPTER 5.
THE ZONE – HOW TO FIND IT, HOW TO STAY THERE LONGER

The Zone is the Holy Grail of golf. It is the magical mix of perfect physical, emotional, and mental balance. It is the natural home of peak performance. Every golfer would like to find the zone more easily, and then learn to stay there longer.

You will almost certainly have experienced the zone many times, but like many people, you did not always recognise it. Whenever you perform any task that you find deeply relaxing, engrossing, and entrancing you have entered the altered mental state known as the zone.

Now you only need to recreate this altered state of mind on the golf course more easily, and then learn to stay there longer.

I will not pretend that finding the zone is easy. It seems a long time ago now but back in December 2007 I spent three days with inspirational golf coach Nick Bradley at his base in Myrtle Beach. We spent most of this time discussing the barriers that the mind can create to either help or hinder our efforts to find the zone.

My career as a doctor in challenging environments was halted prematurely by a neck injury. I felt too young to retire, and enjoyed the opportunity to explore other avenues. On a personal level many of my dreams have since become reality as I discovered how to find the zone more often. As I found the zone I also felt, rightly or wrongly, that I became increasingly lucky. Beset with frustration and mounting bills tested my resolve a lot closer to my limits than I would have chosen. Many times barrier after barrier obstructed my progress as I pursued my dream of being a successful mind coach. However, every time that I was on the verge of giving up Lady Fortune would smile on me. This was all I needed to lift my spirits for a few more weeks.

Since Play Magic Golf was published more than two years ago I have worked almost every day, although watching and coaching golfers in beautiful locations can hardly be described as work. The ultimate challenge for any coach is to work at the top level of golf with tour players, and now I have an increasing number of tour clients.

Victories have followed on the Challenge and Europro tours for my clients, but have eluded them so far on the European Tour, or Big Tour, as it is called. I am firmly convinced that it is only a matter of time, and for a Major victory too. That is the fire that burns even in the darkest hours. A common refrain on the tour is 'I just need a good week!'

Golf encourages dreams, and there is nothing wrong with that. Dreams are a variety of the zone, and dreams or visualisations often lead to unimagined success. The problem is when the dream becomes more important than the process. Doing little things right every day brings results.

So for one reason or another I have been given my opportunity, and that quite simply is all that I asked for. This is the culmination of the long hours of study and work coaching golfers of all shapes, sizes, and abilities. The ultimate challenge.

So I have learnt, with considerable difficulty, to be patient. Success rarely comes overnight. As I say to my clients every day, all things happen at a rate and speed that is appropriate for the individual. It can be tough to follow this advice. To be patient.

In a later chapter we will talk more about the power of giving up, or more accurately letting go, and about how it can counter intuitively create a positive state of mind too. This is when success is least expected, and often surfaces from its hiding place.

Returning to Bradley's words[6],

'However, for some strange reason, this zone is nearly impossible to recreate on a conscious level. The more you try to enter this state, the more elusive it becomes.'

'Less is more' is the way I summarise Nick's observation. The zone lives in the right brain. The more you try to enter it using left brain logic and willpower, the further you move away from it.

Hypnosis

Studying a role model saves enormous time, money, and effort. Until his recent difficulties Tiger Woods was the perfect example of mastering the zone.

At the age of 13 he was introduced to a psychiatrist called Dr. Jay Brunza. There is considerable debate about whether hypnosis formed part of Woods' work with Brunza, or not. It is not important, except to say that many players have used hypnosis, probably with mixed results. So it is a subject that deserves consideration in any book about the power of the mind and golf.

Hypnosis is a much misunderstood subject. At its simplest level it is a process used by a therapist to induce trance. Trance[7] is 'an altered state with an inward focus of attention on a few stimuli.'

I do not consider hypnosis to be a special skill. Indeed I think we all slip in and out of hypnotic states many times every day. The crucial point is that often we do not recognise this, and so fail to appreciate how we could use such experiences to find the zone more easily.

Hypnosis, or more accurately self-hypnosis, can be such a powerful tool for finding the zone it is well worth a few minutes of further reflection.

In 2009 I was invited to write a commentary in the Annual Review of Golf Coaching for a fascinating paper entitled Sport Psychology, Hypnosis and Golf, elegantly written and painstakingly researched by Dr. Simon Jenkins[8].

The following extract from this paper summarises my thoughts then. They are equally valid for the altered mental state that we slip into when absorbed in music, art, dance, or any other similar recreational activity[9].

'It is worth noting that hypnotic processes are ubiquitous in our society, and in history. We are surrounded by hypnotic language in music, poetry, literature (Shakespeare and Dylan Thomas are great examples), and in most circumstances they enrich our culture.

When a mother reads a fairy story to her child in bed she is using hypnotic language, hypnotic imagery, and hypnotic tones. Whether she recognises this or not she knows that this is the best way to relax her child and encourage him or her to fall asleep.

Speech is a relatively recent human evolution. Before its development other sound-based methods of communication would have been an important tool for social cohesion. When a mother makes soothing noises to her crying child she knows instinctively it will calm her child, and perhaps herself too.

Hypnosis might be a relatively simple atavistic evolutionary trait that preceded the development of more complex language skills, and remains more developed (or less latent) in some individuals than others.'

Whether Woods has received coaching in hypnotic techniques is immaterial. What we do know is that Tiger has been brought up as a Buddhist, and that he meditates regularly. We also know that his mental strength is immense, as Craig Perks testifies.

In an extract from a personal note regarding a player we were both coaching at the time (14 October, 2009) Craig wrote,

'To this point, that is why I always emphasize to my high level players, it is imperative that you work diligently on the mental side of the game. Tiger may have the best skill set of anyone who plays at the highest level, what separates him from his peers, is his dominance mentally, it's not even close.'

Craig should know. He held his nerve magnificently to defeat Tiger in the Players Championship in 2002. All the top professionals regard The Players as the fifth Major, so we can be certain that Woods was giving his all to win.

As already described, trance is an altered state with an inward focus of attention on a few stimuli. I regard meditation in the same light. Crucially, both are possible entry points to the zone, because they encourage our thoughts to 'stay in the present.'

If you have discovered your own ways to find the zone – excellent! If not, time spent researching meditation and hypnosis techniques will be invaluable. Without question, your golf will improve as you develop these new skills. Not only that but many other things will improve too, not least your confidence, your communication skills, and your decision-making.

Just as hypnosis is a much misunderstood technique, so too is meditation.

Meditation

There are a wide variety of different meditation techniques. As with hypnosis, many are often packaged as the only definitive method, and enshrine complex prescriptive instructions. It may take years to master these techniques.

However, the truth is that most of us will not spend months and years in deep meditation in search of spiritual enlightenment, laudable as that may be. This is a book about golf, where meditation is just one of the arrows in our quiver to shoot lower scores. So here are a few simple methods to experiment with.

In essence we are looking for a way to connect to our right brain by quietening down our left brain chatter. Whilst ideally we would think of nothing, very few can achieve this goal, so a little direction can be helpful.

Before meditation give your right brain a mission. Keep it simple, and an example might be,

'I am going to enjoy discovering how I can add 30 yards to my drive'.

Or it might be about reading greens more skilfully, whatever is most appropriate for you at the time.

Some people find it helpful to stare at a candle as they drift away; others listen to their favourite chill music, or sit or lie comfortably with their eyes closed. Reciting mantras is another common technique.

A frequent question people ask me is if it matters if they fall asleep during meditation. I think not; the unconscious mind never truly sleeps. As an example many clients who listen to my audiobooks and CDs tell me they have never heard the end of the recording. It does not appear to make any difference to the results.

I have found that gently burning fires, especially camp fires, can also be deeply hypnotic. My eyes defocus without any conscious thought, and lead effortlessly to profound reflection.

I am as certain as I can be that others find the same benefits. All cultures appear to find sitting by fires in contemplation or quiet conversation pleasing. Whilst the security of light and warmth are obvious factors, the dancing flames and embers may work their magic too.

Self-knowledge by definition comes only from inward reflection. Words that others use include daydreaming, meditation, self-hypnosis, prayer, yoga, or visualisation. These methods are all effective entry points to inward reflection. They help us to stay in the present by focusing on our immediate experience. All have their benefits and drawbacks, but each is valid in its own right.

Developing a state of mindfulness is the overarching key to inward reflection. You do not need to practice all the methods listed above. Culture and personal choice dictate which technique is likely to be the most appropriate for the individual at any given time. Clearly one thing is for sure – it will be very difficult, if not impossible, to enter a state of inward reflection without adopting one of these techniques, or the many similar alternatives.

So how can you learn more? The good news is that you are spoilt for choice. Whole books have been written describing each of these examples of mind control. Reassuringly however these techniques are not as difficult to adopt as might be imagined. Courses are readily available in almost all parts of the world, and many of these are now internet based. It is likely to be the best investment in time you can make, and should not be too expensive either. If you are lucky it might even be free.

There are plenty of products to choose from. I recommend as a starting point audiobooks referred to as guided meditations, because they do not require any special training. You do not need to go on a course to experience the still mind that will result from the guided meditation.

I have written another book that delves deeper into these issues. Push at Open Doors discusses how to achieve mindfulness to enter the zone and does not mention golf, but would definitely help any golfer. What works in life usually works on the golf course, and vice versa.

Zen

Zen is a word used many times in relation to golf and rightfully so. Just as with hypnosis and meditation, it has many different definitions.

Zen is a branch of Buddhism, in which meditation forms a central tenet. It is not a religion, but a philosophy. In its purest sense deep insights are transmitted from coach to client not by speech, or words, but by thought. It is like an intuition, instinct, or gut feeling.

Whether this is true or not we all know people that we are comfortable being with, and who make us feel relaxed and confident. We may refer to such people as 'being on the same wavelength.'

Golf is considered a Zen sport, so is archery, swordsmanship, and perhaps even snooker and darts. They are all sports where the control of the mind is a critical success factor for optimum performance.

Zen teaches that a universal human failing is our over-attachment to objects and outcomes. Detachment results in less pressure and greater calm. Missing a short putt does not need to spoil your round, neither will holing it make much difference either. Life by its nature is ebb and flow. Enjoy the good times while they last, and keep your spirits up during the difficult times. They cannot last for ever.

One does not need to be a Buddhist to practice Zen, though we know that Tiger Woods was brought up as one. This is almost certainly one of the factors responsible for his success, and may prove critical in his rehabilitation as he attempts to return to his roots. During 2009 it was evident from his body language and the tone of his interviews that all was not well. He had strayed from Zen, and was already paying a heavy price for it.

We do not need to become Buddhists like Tiger. For the rest of us all that is necessary to improve our golf is to follow selectively some key Zen principles. This book is full of them. If you wish to read more about this fascinating subject I recommend an excellent review article, Zen Buddhism, Sport Psychology and Golf[10].

Happiness

I mentioned earlier that happiness is the emotion I consider most valuable on the golf course. We all want more happiness in our lives, and just as with the zone, the more we want it, the more elusive it becomes.

During my time in Africa I was surprised to discover that happiness can be found in the most unlikely places, such as in refugee camps, the orphans homes, and on the streets with the homeless. I am not suggesting for a moment that these are not terrible places to live, rather that even in such abject poverty fleeting moments of happiness can be found. It is probably the most valuable resource needed to survive, after warmth, shelter, food, and water.

Curiously happiness is sometimes less easy to find amongst the rich and privileged, or even on the golf course. In following chapters we will talk about confidence and visualisation. Clients often tell me they have been taught these subjects, but not been shown how to be confident, or how to develop visualisations.

So it is with happiness. How can we find more happiness in our lives? As with all things, we can learn what makes people happy by studying happy people, or more accurately, by studying what they are doing when they feel happy.

Happiness is an emotion which at its most fundamental level is due to the effects of various neurotransmitter chemicals manufactured within the body. We have already mentioned several of them, and another group are the opioid peptides called endorphins.

Endorphins were so named because their chemical structure closely resembles the synthetic drug morphine. The 'endo' part of their name simply means they are manufactured within the body.

Endorphins have been suggested as the chemicals released by long distance runners that gets them through 'The Wall', that produce pain relief during acupuncture, and that contribute to a sense of well-being through pregnancy.

They also make people feel happy. Happy people make better golfers. Justin Rose, a former client of Nick Bradley, is a perfect example of this. He wrote after his maiden victory on the US Tour in June 2010[11],

'The crazy thing is that when you are in the bubble, you are not really conscious of what you are doing — so it feels relatively easy.

The key was to not chase it. I have finally got to the point where I am telling myself just to enjoy the game. Play it for what it is and don't fret about the results. In that way, I have discarded quite a bit of baggage.'

Much of the rest of this book will show you in one way or another how to bring a little more happiness into your golf, and your life. Happiness is an emotion, so to a greater or lesser extent you can learn how to control it. A little more goes a long way.

More than two thousand years ago Aristotle also concluded that all people want happiness. Happiness cannot be seen in isolation, but measured in the context of a whole life. He described it thus[12],

'One swallow does not make a summer, nor does one happy day guarantee a happy life.'

Professor Csikszentmihalyi describes happiness as a 'flow experience[13].' He studied thousands of people at work and in their leisure time. He found that people were most happy when completely absorbed in whatever they were doing. It could be complex surgery, or something far more mundane – the level of happiness was the same.

Csikszentmihalyi also considers his flow experience to be identical to that experienced by musicians in the groove, or athletes in the zone. Surely proof, if any further proof is required, that a little more happiness in our lives will translate to a lot lower scores on the golf course.

Three Quantum Laws Of Golf – The Proven 3QL System

I did warn at the outset that this book involved a personal journey for both writer and reader. It would have saved much time to fast forward to this page, where I finally introduce the 3 Quantum Laws Of Golf.

Sadly, this would not have been possible. Whilst the 3QL system is effective as a stand-alone coaching process, its effect is multiplied many times over by even a superficial understanding of its origins and foundations.

Another reward for your reflections thus far is that the previous chapters can also be read in isolation on their own merit. Some of the currency of your golfing advancement is in the bank already. It can only get better.

The 3 Quantum Laws Of Golf is the foundation of my coaching approach to clients. It has worked for thousands of golfers and non-golfers alike, and will work for you. It is highly likely that you will discover at least one nugget that will improve your golf. All I ask for is an open mind, and a commitment to experiment with a different approach. Then I am as sure as I can be that all will be well.

Meditation Booth

Three Nuggets For Now

1.

2.

3.

CHAPTER 6.
1st QUANTUM LAW – TALK TENDERLY – HOW TO SILENCE SELF-DOUBT

If I were only given one minute with a golfer this would be my first lesson, and will immediately cut shots off their score. If, that is, the golfer would keep quiet for long enough to listen. It concerns their internal dialogue.

These are the voices that we all have in our brains. There is often a constant chatter giving a running commentary of our life. Very often it slips out of the mouth, usually followed by an embarrassed pause. 'I was just talking to myself', we explain.

These are our superficial thoughts. Deeper thoughts are probably non-verbal, and we will consider these later.

Your Thoughts Control Your Mood

One of the phrases I repeat time after time to my clients is so simple, yet so fundamental to golf. Even the pros sometimes get it wrong.

'What goes on in your head comes out on the golf course.'

I will explain what I mean by this. We have already considered the nature of thought. So little is understood, but it does appear that complex brain chemicals are involved somewhere.

Think of a visit to the dentist, chemicals are released in your brain, and you have a bad feeling in your stomach. Well, most people do, although there are some strange folk who look forward to their dental appointment.

So let us return to the example. You have a bad feeling about your visit to the dentist tomorrow. Yet it has not happened, it is all in your imagination. This is a demonstration of how thoughts influence emotions, and how emotions influence the physiology of our bodies.

We have unearthed another glittering key. It is one of the most important buried treasures we desire – control. Now we just need to learn how to use it. Professor Csikszentmihalyi has researched this subject widely.

'The simple truth – that the control of consciousness determines the quality of life – has been known for a long time; in fact, for as long as human records exist.[13]'

Most dentists are very good at what they do, and cause little if any pain to their patients. Again perception is stronger than reality, and so we still have the same unpleasant feeling in our stomach.

There are more helpful ways to think of our dental appointment. Look upon it as an opportunity to lie back for a few minutes, close our eyes, no need to make conversation, no phone calls, texts, or emails to distract us, and an opportunity to meditate. It is a chance to think of our last holiday, a fun evening with friends, to visualise our shopping trip, to ponder what to prepare for the evening meal.

These thoughts release different chemicals, and the resultant feelings are far more pleasant. We have not changed reality. We are still thinking of our dental appointment. We have changed our perception, and thus how we feel about it. We have demonstrated that we can control to some extent our thoughts, emotions, and the effect these have on our bodies.

We can use this on the golf course too. This is such an empowering technique that we will revisit it many times in the following chapters.

Stop Beating Yourself Up

Now I will return to what goes on in your head comes out on the golf course. This is even more valid when what goes on in the head comes out of the mouth. A few more million brain cells have exerted their influence on your idle chatter. So it is a good idea to be very careful of your thoughts, and especially what you say.

I continue to hear so many destructive things said by a person about his or her golf, and about themselves. The brain is not stupid - if it hears bad things about itself it will start to believe them, and this will lead to poor self-esteem, and a downward spiral of a self-fulfilling prophecy.

I love the practice ground. I enjoy practicing golf more than playing, and time flies. It is also my office, and my laboratory too. I can observe my subjects at my leisure.

One day I thought I was alone, when I heard a shout. I looked around. About 100 metres away a solitary golfer was smashing his way through his basket of practice balls. Almost every shot was followed by an oath or shout of disgust.

I was fascinated. I edged closer. Every so often a club would be thrown; sometimes the bag would be hit. Poor bag, what had it done wrong? By now I could hardly control my amusement.

The final straw was when the golfer threw his club to the ground for the last time, stood with legs apart and arms outstretched to the heavens, part in anger, part in supplication, and screamed.

I stopped laughing; this was not funny anymore. Worse was to come. I noticed for the first time the practice ground attendant calmly about his duties, collecting balls, and repairing divots.

The attendant was totally oblivious of this demented behaviour. He saw and heard this kind of performance almost every day, and thought it was normal. Not for the first time I asked myself,

'Is golf a sport, or is it an obsession, a compulsion, or even an addiction?'

How To Talk Yourself Out Of A Great Score
I listen to golfers on the practice ground, on the practice putting green, and waiting on the first tee. Many have talked themselves out of a good round before they have even started.

These are just a few examples of unskilful comments I hear every day. I am sure you will have heard similar, and can add to the list.

- I wish I'd missed that practice putt, and saved it for the round.
- I hate this hole, I never make par.
- I always put my drive in that pond.
- The greens are terrible today; I'll never make a putt.
- The sand in the bunker is impossible to get out of.

I hear many other damaging self directed comments during the round too. Usually I choose to ignore them, but sometimes I find it hard to remain silent.

'How would you feel if another person said to you what you have just said to yourself?'

They reply,

'I never would use bad language to others. I respect people, and they would be very offended if I did talk to them like that. I expect others to show me the same respect.'

At this stage in the conversation I have usually made my point. Rarely is it necessary to finish with,

'Then why do you say that to yourself?

If You Can't Think Of Anything Good To Say, Then Say Nothing

The way we think about ourselves is very important. This next bit is a diamond. Make it your mantra.

'From this moment forward I will never say a bad thing about myself again.'

Every client is different, and every seminar group similarly so. That is what makes my job so interesting. Some readily embrace this concept of universal self-worth, others struggle with it.

The group that have expressed the strongest reservations to date were a group of talented Juniors, aged 12-16. They were concerned that if they followed my suggestion it could make them arrogant, or appear so.

That is a very valid point, and we debated it at length. My view is that the unconscious mind knows very well when we have screwed up, and digests the lessons for the future. Certainly if others have been hurt by our unhelpful actions then sincere apologies are the minimum redress required.

Others have expressed reservations that concern the danger that we may lose out on the opportunity to learn from our mistakes. So I often add the following words to the mantra.

'Fear not. You can trust family, friends, and the rest of the world to point out your mistakes for you. You do not need to give them any help.'

Why positive internal dialogue is so important is simple. If you only say good things to yourself you will feel happier and more confident, and make better decisions.

If you can remember a favourite teacher from your past the chances are that teacher was very kind, gave much praise, awarded high marks, and created an atmosphere of relaxation and trust in the classroom. That is when people learn the easy way. It is also when people find their zone, and perform at a much higher level, on and off the golf course.

Some readers have gently reprimanded me about the above mantra too. Their concern is that it is expressed negatively, i.e 'I will NEVER say....' They are correct because this is a golden rule in self development, and I am still puzzled why I expressed it in this way. For some reason I like it. However, try this option too, and see which one you prefer.

'From this moment forward I will always say good things about myself.'

Mind Your Words
Milton Erickson, psychiatrist and father of American Medical Hypnosis was once asked,

'Are you aware of the way in which you use your words?'

He replied:

'I certainly am, and I want to emphasise the importance of that awareness in all of you. In any work, you are going to use words to influence the psychological life of an individual today; you are going to use words to influence his organic life today; you are going to also influence his psychological and organic life twenty years from now.

So you had better know what you are saying. You had better be willing to reflect upon the words you use, to wonder what their meanings are, and to seek out and understand their many associations.'

These profound comments apply equally to the words that we use in our head about ourselves. I cannot overemphasise how important they are to the way we play and enjoy our golf, and ultimately the scores we shoot.

The language patterns we use are also important and I will give you an example. During my golf seminars I walk a few holes with each delegate. On the first tee I ask them to describe their thoughts to me, and they are usually illuminating. This would be a typical example of unskilful dialogue.

'I can see out of bounds on the right and my ball must not go there. On the left there is a large bunker and so I must not go there either. So I'm going to try and hit the ball down the middle.'

Unfortunately for this golfer their ball is highly unlikely to find the fairway, and for this reason. When you give an order to a child, what are the chances of it being followed? They are usually not very high.

There is something very contrary about our brains, and not just in children. Imperative words such as 'must', and 'insist', usually lead to passive resistance at best. In grammatical terms these words are referred to as modal operators of necessity.

Words that are modal operators of possibility are far more attractive to our right brain. So with the example that I gave a moment ago my reframe would be simple.

'I am choosing to enjoy hitting the ball exactly there, at the top branch of that tall tree.'

Another interesting point is that the right brain does not appear to recognise the words 'No' and 'Not' when we think of hazards. Even the word 'hazard' rings alarm bells. This is why when we think, 'Do not go in the bunker' we usually end up right there.

In the past I have caddied for friends on the PGA European and Seniors Tour. My first experience illustrated some of these points perfectly.

A fellow caddie was trying to be helpful to his player by pointing out the white markers that delineated out of bounds, and the bunkers on the other side of the fairway.

His player went ballistic, and told his caddy to shut up right now because he was 'doing my head in!'

Players are only interested in their target line, and carry distances. If a bunker is on their line, but under their carry distance it simply does not exist. We would do well to think likewise.

Change The Voice In Your Head

Not only are the words we use important, but also the voice with which we use them. Despite my years of meditation and hypnosis experience I struggled with self-hypnosis.

In 2008 I attended an exclusive three-day course with a hypnosis guru, and this was one of my ten key questions I had prepared to ask him. The course was expensive, but worth every penny. Dr. Richard Bandler is considered by many to be the World's best hypnotist, and Paul McKenna considers him to be his guru too. That is how good he is.

Richard considered my question for a few seconds. His answer took even less time. To be exact his answer was a question too.

'When you are attempting self-hypnosis whose voice specifically do you use?'

I immediately knew the answer, and kicked myself. I realised instantly that our brains generally do not listen to our own voice, especially when it attempts to give direction. We hear our voice all the time, and whilst we love to hear it, familiarity can certainly lead to boredom.

It is far better to choose another voice. Some of my best rounds of golf or most creative moments have been with my coach, or a friend, metaphorically whispering advice in my ear. It does not have to be the same person every time, sometimes there is even more than one person.

I have passed on this simple but priceless lesson to my clients, and many have found it extremely powerful. There is one group who sometimes struggle with it – the medical doctors.

Doctors are generally wonderful and caring people. Unfortunately some are also full of powerful negative thoughts. This is not surprising. They see the effects of disease on their patients every day.

The reason some doctors struggle with voices in their heads is because they know that this can be one of the first rank symptoms of schizophrenia. This is correct. However there is one critical difference. Schizophrenics cannot control their voices, whilst I can. I can choose whichever voice I like, when I like, and make it go away whenever I choose too. I think most other people can do likewise.

So I encourage the good doctors to stick with their own voice if they prefer. I would give the same advice to anybody else too if they feel uncomfortable with the other voice, or 'voices in their head' concept.

We will now return full circle to the mantra I suggested to you at the beginning of this chapter.

'From this moment forward I will never say a bad thing about myself again. '

This is the 1st Quantum Law. It sounds simple, and it is. However you have learnt unhelpful dialogue over many years, so it will take some conscious effort before you unconsciously learn how to talk tenderly to yourself all the time. In the next chapter we will discover the joy and awesome power of being able to turn on the confidence tap whenever we need some extra help.

Meditation Booth

Three Nuggets For Now
1.

2.

3.

CHAPTER 7.
2ND QUANTUM LAW – CREATE CONFIDENTLY – HOW TO TURN ON THE CONFIDENCE TAP

Confidence is critical to playing great golf. Some days we have it, other days we do not, and it is tantalisingly difficult to explain why this should be so.

Confidence is the foundation that we build the rest of our lives around. Confident people do not worry about the past, and become depressed – nor do they worry about the future, and become anxious, and develop panic attacks.

Confident people achieve great things, they attract many friends, and they relish dealing with problems – they see them just as exciting challenges to overcome. They play great golf too.

My clients present with a wide variety of issues. I see many non-golfers too. Doctors learn early in their careers that the presenting symptom is usually just the superficial expression of a deeper concern. Further exploration is required to correctly identify the underlying issue. In almost all cases an underlying lack of confidence is a significant finding, either as a cause, or a result of other issues. So far no client has ever asked me to make them less confident.

If you check the iTunes audiobook charts you will see many titles related to confidence. These charts are an accurate reflection of what topics occupy our minds at any time. I am as certain as I can be that apart from technical ability confidence is the single most important resource for golfers.

When we do anything different such as speaking in public, or performing in the sports arena, we need to harness our skills and find what is called a resourceful state, and one of these resources would include confidence. So how can you be more confident when under pressure?

As usual you do not need to reinvent any more wheels. It is much easier to learn from people who found ways to create confidence on demand.

Memory – Tidy Up The Filing Cabinet

The brain has a complex filing system, and processes many millions of bits of information every day. This creates its own problems, as information has to be processed. At the simplest level it is either stored or discarded.

The brain appears to save all or almost all of this information. This in turn creates even more work because the information has to be catalogued. Generally recent important information has a higher priority than older unimportant information. Information relating to danger also has a higher priority than that related to pleasure.

Whether this is genetic programming or learned behaviour is unclear. However the result in modern life is that too much thought focuses on negative rather than positive events.

As an example I know from my seminars that people can remember five bad experiences during a day much more easily than five good ones. As a result this behaviour conditions the brain over time to a more negative mind set than desirable.

During most of my career I worked in the developing world. I was surrounded by life and death challenges, with few tried and trusted methods to guide me. As my experience grew over the years I found myself less and less involved in hands-on medicine, and more involved in developing teams. Teams move a lot slower than individuals, and building consensus for a new project requires considerable patience. I soon discovered an invaluable short cut.

Deal with the negatives first, move on, and then woo the imagination with the intriguing possibilities. In other words encourage the team to move from left to right brain thinking.

This is how it works. The team assemble for the day. As facilitator and team leader my role is to coordinate and not to direct the process. The team objective is to construct and operate a hospital in a rural community in Africa. Just to make it even more challenging the civil war is raging too.

My opening comments to the team are not,

'How are we going to construct and operate a hospital in a rural community in Africa?'

Instead my opening comments are,

'What are the reasons why we cannot construct and operate a hospital in a rural community in Africa?'

The walls of the conference room were soon covered with flip chart notes. After about two hours we had all but exhausted the reasons why this plane was not going to fly.

After a short break it was time for a different approach. I can't remember exactly what I said, but it would have followed along these lines.

'You have been selected for this task force because of your leadership qualities, and your proven track record of delivering outstanding results in the most challenging environments.

You have shown on many occasions that the impossible is often the untried. I do not believe that on these walls covered in our charts we cannot find just one of these problems that we can't solve.'

Heads tilt, eyes move in different directions, and I know their right brains are looking at the problem, literally from all directions. I also know then that the project has launched, and the plane has lurched into the air, against all the odds. There will be much more trial and tribulation to come, but with the right balance of people, money, and other stuff the hospital will happen.

The hospital project was a complex example of negativity at work, and how this energy can be redirected. Similar examples happen to us every day. Brain misfiling is relatively common.

Trivial negative events from the past may be assigned far more importance than they deserve, and in extreme cases can be emotionally crippling, as in phobias. Apparently when we are born we are only frightened by two things; loud noises and falling. We spend the rest of our lives adding to this list, often inappropriately.

The reason I mention the hospital project is because you might like to adopt the same approach with your golf. Confront the negativity and stare it down. If your current handicap is 20 make your goal 9. Impossible? Write down all the reasons why it would be impossible to play to 9. If your handicap is 10 make scratch your goal.

When you have run out of reasons take a break. Have a look at your list the following day and choose the easiest point to attack. Now you have started. I still remember the sagely words of my rugby coach at school – the hardest part of practice is putting your boots on. Momentum builds after the first step. Now you know that your goal is at least possible, whereas just a day ago it was impossible. You have made a huge leap forward just by playing with words.

Self-limiting Beliefs – Bin Them

Almost all of us are held back by the past. More accurately by how we feel about the past. This can create a real obstacle to fulfilling our potential. Fortunately there are tools and tips to overcome self-limiting beliefs.

Sometimes it is the smallest things can continue to hold us back. Many of these beliefs originate from comments made to us by teachers, parents, or other authority figures from years ago. Often these comments tell us that we will never be good at music, or art, or sport, or languages, and all manner of other things. Even worse is when such comments are directed at our physical appearance.

These are all self-limiting beliefs that we no longer need, and never did. The truth is that everybody can be good at all of these things, when approached in the right way. Whilst we cannot change the things that have happened in the past, we can certainly discover how to change the way we think about them.

I know this to be true. When I work as a member of the training team with Richard Bandler and Paul McKenna I see examples of ordinary people producing art, playing an instrument in tune, speaking in a foreign language, and delivering a short speech in public. These are all things that they had been told as a child, and continued to believe as an adult, that would be impossible for them.

Whilst their results do not usually reach professional standard they are certainly more than adequate, and display a lot more competence than they ever thought they possessed, or were possible. These were all skills they were told they did not have, and never would. It did not take hours of counselling to overcome this lack of belief, only about thirty minutes. The short cut was hypnosis, which was able to bypass the blocks, and constituted a direct appeal to the right brain.

I think I have given enough examples of how confidence, or rather the lack of it, limits our performance at golf, and in our wider life. Now it is time to do something about it.

Confidence Anchors – How To Hang On To Those Great Memories

People often ask me,

'How can I feel more confident when I'm about to play a difficult shot, or I feel overawed by my playing partners?'

Well, there is a way we can tap into instant confidence and this is how you can do it.

As with most things in life it will require some preparation, and effort on your part. However in relation to the size of the glittering prize out there it will be one of the best investments you have ever made.

From this moment forward remember every good thing that happens to you. Unfortunately most people have a brilliant memory at remembering all the things that went wrong, but struggle to think of the many good things that have gone right.

So when somebody gives you a compliment, wallow in the pleasure for a second or two longer than you ordinarily would, before allowing the memory to slip into your unconscious mind.

When you hit a great shot capture as much detail as you can, and savour every morsel. This is a simple way to give the brain a little direction. Your message to your brain goes something like this.

'I like this feeling, so store this memory in a place where I can find it more easily.'

If you can do this several times a day for a month there will be a subtle change in your brain chemistry and outlook on life. You will notice the difference. Those closest to you will notice it more.

You can enhance the effect by subtly giving your brain another push in the right (brain) direction. This will turbo boost the positive effect. This is how you do it.

When you have one of these pleasurable experiences make sure that the memory is easy to retrieve by associating it with a physical anchor. This is the equivalent to the brain of bold underline formatting in your brightest and favourite colour.

Some people touch their thumb and forefinger together as a physical anchor to reinforce a happy memory. Others touch their ear, or brush their trousers. Spend some time choosing your anchor. It should be discreet, but most importantly it should feel right with you.

You probably already have an anchor, but do not realise it. When I watch clients hit shots I can usually identify their anchor within a couple of minutes. If you can spot your anchor and it works for you do not change it.

If you watch professional entertainers and athletes you will be able to spot their confidence anchors too, and see how they seamlessly form part of their routine. A great way to improve your skills at body watching is to watch TV, but with the sound muted.

Confidence Triggers – Load, Aim, and Fire – The Power of the Little Red Dot

Once you have built powerful confidence anchors, you are ready for the next step. This is how it works. If you have reinforced ten positive things every day for a week, or a month, or even years your brain will recognise the physical anchor as a good thing happening.

So just consider this for a moment. How do you think your brain would feel when you are about to play a tricky bunker shot if you fired off your confidence anchor before you played the shot?

This is the confidence trigger. The brain recalls happy memories, of things going right, and this gives an instant buzz of confidence. At a deep unconscious level your brain believes it has already played this magical shot.

Suddenly the chances of you making a great sand save have increased enormously. Try it and see, and the great news is that it works for many other things than golf.

Another way to build a confidence anchor is to think of a time when you were very confident – it could be a time when you played one of your best rounds ever, when the right words came as if by magic, or when you felt especially creative – the example doesn't really matter, because it is the feeling that is important.

So when you need instant confidence recall this memory, and the endorphins will start to flow. Now you will have a great feeling, and much more confidence, and the anxieties will fade away.

Even pulling your club out of the bag can be a powerful confidence anchor. Think of the best ever shot you have played with each club in as much detail as possible. Remember that writing is the doing part of thinking, so write it down. Make it your habit that when you touch each club you instantly remember the best ever shot you made with it.

2010 Open champion Louis Oosthuizen used a little red dot as his confidence trigger[14]. It helped him to stay in the present.

'A small red spot on the glove of golfer Louis Oosthuizen is credited with playing a critical role in his winning of The Open Championship at St Andrews last Sunday. The coloured spot was a visible manifestation of the growing influence of psychology in sport – it was designed to help the 27-year-old South African concentrate on his swing in the crucial moments leading up to a shot.

Sporting professionals are increasingly turning to similar mind-training tricks to improve their performance on the field. It may involve mental imagery that allows them to rehearse a game in their heads, or psychological blocking techniques that stop them from dwelling on past mistakes. In the case of Oosthuizen, an outsider who was widely expected to collapse under the pressure on the final day, it was a simple dot on his glove to make him focus on his swing.'

It worked for Louis; it will work for you too. The effort you invest in creating and reinforcing your anchors will be repaid many times over as your confidence grows.

Louis's mind coach was Dr. Karl Morris. Since I wrote the first edition of Play Magic Golf I have enjoyed training with Karl, and am now one of his Master Coaches. He has told me more details about the little red dot story, and I believe it to be a cracking example of how psychological methods can be ingeniously adapted to produce stunning results. Here are some additional details.

Louis was a surprise Open contender, and widely expected to crumble on the final day. Well, as you know, he didn't, and everybody else did. We will never know how much was due to the red dot, but my guess is that it was instrumental.

Louis's objective that week was not to win The Open (no pressure!), but to follow his pre-shot routine perfectly on every hole, and execute his technique. On almost every hole he succeeded, and guess what? The score took care of itself! Where have you heard that before?

So how did Louis keep his focus? Karl and Louis sat down together before the tournament, and Karl asked him to remember the best round he had played this year. That bit was easy. Then Karl asked him to describe in one word how he felt during this round.

'Concentration.'

The next question was the bit that I couldn't work out.

'If concentration had a colour, what would that colour be?'

The answer was red, and that surprised me. What a powerful example! As coaches we must always keep in mind that the client chooses. For sure we would never have chosen red. This is only my guess but I think Louis chose red because this colour wakes him up, and stops his concentration drifting elsewhere.

I have used this technique in different ways with many of my clients. It has been successful in playing professional poker, taking examinations, public speaking, as well as golf. My suggestion is to reflect deeply on this little story, and consider how you could use it. It could help you a lot, and not just in golf.

No Escape From Success – Why Would You Want To?

It is a great idea to keep reminding your right brain of what you are good at to boost your long-term self-esteem. Writing is the doing part of thinking, so jot down some key bullet points. Perhaps they are your best ever shots, perhaps your best shots on your last round. Write them on a piece of paper or on your computer and print them out. Keep this piece of paper close to you. In a place where you can see it every day, and use it to remind yourself of the great choices you have made.

Supermodels and Martial Arts – Learn From The Tough Guys

Body language is another way to build confidence. Models are taught early in their careers to 'Look Up.' You will also benefit from standing tall, being aware of the way you walk, being aware of your slow and controlled breathing, being aware of being happy, of smiling from the inside, and of being comfortable in your own skin, the state of mind we call 'Inner Confidence'.

A friend of mine, Michele, was a supermodel, and now works as a TV confidence coach for models.

'Own the room, you bitch!' she remembers being shouted at her, when she was a shy girl trying to be as small as possible in front of the cameras. It is a tough life being a model, and the point of Michele's story is that posture is not everything to confidence, but it comes close.

Practitioners of martial arts discover the ageless wisdom of 'Holding a Point.' They learn how to move their energy from their busy mind to a point in their low abdomen, close to their centre of gravity. This produces a feeling of a still mind, confidence, calm, detachment, and great strength.

You can experiment with this, and it is most enlightening when done with a friend. Please be very, very careful and gentle with the following exercise. Choose a safe open area, for obvious safety reasons.

Stand comfortably with your legs slightly apart. Ask your friend to touch your shoulder, and gently push you. Keep your balance.

Then close your eyes, and focus your thoughts low in your stomach. Feel as if this point is your centre of gravity, and that you are strongly grounded. Ask your friend to gently push you again. This time you will move less, and your friend will notice the change. This exercise can be quite dramatic, and the result improves with practice.

By the simple act of thinking of these things your perception has already started to shift. The more you practice developing a confident posture, the better and more easily you will find these feelings. This is yet another route to the confident place that athletes call the zone.

Here is yet another example. Imagine a person who is very nervous, perhaps the same patient I mentioned earlier waiting at the clinic to see the dentist. Let's examine the body language.

He or she is likely to be shrunk into the seat, arms and legs crossed, head and eyes downcast, perhaps we can make out a film of perspiration on the top lip, or even 'saddlebags' across the chest and under the arms. The person is breathing fast and shallow, and their hands are trembling. If we hooked the patient up to a monitor we would record a fast pulse rate, and perhaps a raised blood pressure too.

These are all physiological responses to an event that has not even happened. The thought is enough to release chemicals such as adrenaline, which produces this response. It is called the 'fight or flight' reaction. It might be appropriate if we are about to be attacked by a lion, but not of much use in the dentist's clinic. Unless we want to run home or attack the dentist!

I think we can all agree that these feelings are great for fighting lions and dentists, but the last thing we need on the golf course. So what can we do about it?

Fake It Until You Make It

This is another favourite expression from my supermodel friend Michele. Go back to the nervous person waiting for the dentist. This time we will change the body language. Sit tall, lean slightly forward, head up and still, eyes engaged with target, legs slightly apart, arms slightly apart from the body, (described by actors as 'air under the armpit'), and breathe slowly and deeply.

This works. All we have changed is our posture. Control of breathing is another powerful technique, and we will discuss it in more detail in a later chapter. It is difficult to be calm when breathing fast, and consequently difficult to feel nervous when breathing slowly.

Another friend, Tony, is a TV presenter, and on camera for several hours a day. He knows the importance of a confident posture, and works hard at developing it for two reasons.

First, good posture looks good on TV. We do not want to invite people into our sitting room who look nervous and sweaty.

Second, it makes Tony the presenter feel more confident too. Just by changing his posture.

You have guessed correctly; good posture works well on the golf course too. I sometimes work with another friend and golf coach Mark. He puts a high value on body language too. He coaches golfers to walk like a predator, especially on the putting green. Walk lightly in perfect balance, eyes never leaving the target, ready to throw the spear at any moment. It might sound fanciful, but it works. Try it and see.

Preparation And 'The Long Walk'

Helpful preparation is also a very important part of positioning yourself for success, or at least giving you the greatest possible chance of success. Again, we can learn from others.

The great Elvis Presley suffered from anxiety before major performances. His team would place his trailer exactly 1000 yards from the stage. My guess is that as he applied his stage make-up, and then selected his costume, he came closer to being 'The King' who had enormous charisma and massive confidence.

As Elvis left his caravan and heard the crowds every step was taking him closer to the stage. By the time he took his final step he had changed from being an anxious individual into being this other person - one of the greatest entertainers of all time.

Your mental and physical preparation for golf is equally important. Allow sufficient time for travel, practice, and 'tuning in' to the golf course. If you drive to the venue focus on driving smoothly, listening to relaxing music. On arrival be equally smooth in your movements. Spend some time finding your way around, identifying the locker room, practice area, and the first tee.

Circle Of Certainty

We expect airline pilots to plan their route and alternate destinations in advance, rather than make decisions impulsively. If something unexpected happens they are already prepared, and have the confidence to deal with it.

So it is with golf, and this example illustrates the point perfectly. Imagine a circle around the ball several feet in diameter. Leave your bag outside the circle. Do not enter 'The Circle of Certainty' until you have decided on your shot.

In other words consider wind, slope, distance, carry, and club selection before you enter the circle and start your pre-shot routine. It is the same with putting.

If you are distracted within the Circle or still have doubts come out and start again. This may irritate your playing partners, but will save you many shots. Inside the circle your thoughts are certain, and so there is no room for doubt.

How many times after a bad shot do you hear the familiar refrain,

'I knew I was going to do that!'

So don't do it. Simple?

In the next Chapter you will have an opportunity to be a great movie director. Forget the credit crunch, your budget is unlimited. You can hire the best actors, camera and sound technicians, special effects wizards, and travel to the most exotic locations.

How good does that make you feel?

Meditation Booth

Three Nuggets For Now
1.

2.

3.

CHAPTER 8.
3RD QUANTUM LAW – MAKE MOVIES MAGICALLY – HOW TO VISUALISE THE SHOT OF YOUR DREAMS

Learn From The Greatest Living Golfer – Jack Nicklaus

One man truly understood the power of visualisation – Jack Nicklaus. He worked this out for himself long before the armies of psychologists arrived on the golf scene. Let me give you one of his examples from his book Golf My Way[15].

'I never hit a shot, not even in practice, without having a very sharp, in-focus picture of it in my head. It's like a colour movie.

First I 'see' where I want it to finish, nice and white and sitting up high on the bright green grass.

Then the scene quickly changes and I 'see' the ball going there: its path, trajectory, and shape, even its behaviour on landing.

Then there is this sort of fadeout, and the next scene shows me making the kind of swing that will turn the previous images to reality.'

How many golfers exercise this degree of thought to every shot they hit – even in practice? I know that very few do. Reflect again on Jack's mental imagery, think how you can use it for your game, and cut several shots off your score immediately.

We can learn even more from Jack. When Nicklaus retired to his room in the evening, he referred to going to the movies. He would lie on his bed and replay his round, examining each shot, making edits, and finally watching his perfect movie.

As a result he would have real difficulty remembering the bad shots, because in his mind they had not happened, nor had they left a negative imprint behind. Not surprisingly, he would construct a perfect movie of the next day too.

Tiger Woods is another example of a great golfer with superb visualisation skills. Rather than spending all his time on the practice area, he now puts more time aside for mental reflection, visualising in his mind how he wants to swing the club. This mental picture helps him relate his golf swing to the overall movement of his body.

Dr. Simon Jenkins (Principal Lecturer in Sports Coaching) describes mental practice as[16],

'Covert (rather than overt) practice of a skill in that no actual movement occurs. It involves the use of imagery and verbal thoughts.'

Skiers do the same too. Physiologists have wired their muscles, and attached them to recording machines. This is called electromyography. They discovered that when a skier is standing in the laboratory with eyes closed visualising their next competition run the same muscle groups are being flexed, and at the same time, as would happen on the real run, mirroring the ski terrain.

Jenkins confirms the value of mental practice too from a scientific standpoint.

'There is evidence to suggest that mental practice is better than no practice, and that mental practice in combination with physical practice is even better.'

This is good news for those who spend long days away from home, or who live in inhospitable climates. Play golf in your mind. If you are not yet convinced then this famous example may be the final convincer. It was written by Hirini Reedy, and is also quoted by Csikszentmihalyi[13.]

'Major James Nesbeth spent seven years as a prisoner of war in North Vietnam. During those seven years, he was imprisoned in a cage that was approximately four and one-half feet high and five long. During almost the entire time he was imprisoned he saw no one, talked to no one and experienced no physical activity. In order to keep his sanity and his mind active, he used the art of visualization.

Every day in his mind, he would play a game of golf. A full 18-hole game at his favorite green. In his mind, he would create the trees, the smell of the freshly trimmed grass, the wind, the songs of the birds. He created different weather conditions - windy spring days, overcast winter days and sunny summer mornings. He felt the grip of the club in his hands as he played his shots in his mind. The set-up, the down-swing and the follow-through on each shot. Watched the ball arc down the fairway and land at the exact spot he had selected. All in his mind. He did this seven days a week. Four hours a day. Eighteen holes. Seven years. When Major Nesbeth was finally released, he found that he had cut 20 strokes off his golfing average without having touched a golf club in seven years.'

Other top golfers run their movies too, although thankfully in less harsh circumstances. They prolong their pre-shot routine until they feel ready to hit the ball. They might wait until in their movie the hole gets closer, or the fairway gets wider, or the green gets bigger. Perhaps they have found their own hypnotic induction that works for them. One thing is for sure - they do not hit the ball until they are ready – and neither should you.

Putt For Dough – Fix An Elastic Band To Your Putter

Now you can start to develop your creative right brain too. This will be easy for some, and just a little more of a challenge for others. It does not matter. You do not need to become a total right brain person; all that is necessary is to make a shift from left to right. This alone will also cut shots off your score, and make you a better golfer.

Let me give you an example of a simple visualisation that others have found helpful. The video clip I filmed of this technique proved popular with viewers on YouTube. Clients often consult me when they are having problems sinking pressure putts. The top golfers all have very different putting styles. That tells me that one size definitely does not fit all, and most pros agree that the mental approach to putting is far more important than any technical skill. Putting guru Dave Stockton certainly thinks so too, and his clients include many of the top names in golf.

The visualisation technique I mentioned is to ask clients to imagine that a rubber band stretches from the centre of the hole to the middle of their putter blade. As they move the putter backwards and forwards they feel, with a little right brain shift, the tension in the rubber band pulling the blade towards the hole.

Try it with your eyes closed and you'll see what I mean. This is a very good technique for improving the distance and direction of your putts. It also gives a much smoother putting action because the stretching of elastic by definition is very smooth.

Make Sense Of Your Five Senses – Go Large With Your Movie

Great movie directors know the importance of creating vivid imagery using all our senses. These are our only information inputs from our environment – an environment that is limitless in its abundant diversity. These senses are all we have to make sense of our surroundings, and everything is channelled through these conduits.

We have five senses; what we see, hear, feel, taste, and smell. Now it is time for you to direct your own movie. Make sure it is packed with detail relating to your five senses.

So let us get the cameras rolling. Lie back, close your eyes, and imagine some competition in the future, perhaps a few months away, a competition that you would like to win.

Picture yourself receiving the trophy or the prize, and being asked to deliver the customary modest but eloquent winner's speech. Then reflect on all the things that went right over the preceding months to position you for your success in the competition. You recognise that your processes were sound, and that your journey was a series of small steps, and not all of them were in the correct direction, or so it seemed at the time.

Your thoughts are interrupted as a journalist from the local paper approaches you and asks you for the secret of the amazing improvement in your game. Could you pass on some tips that would interest and help her readers?

Pause for thought for a few seconds. Then share with her some of the most illuminating insights and suggestions that you found the most useful in winning this competition. Most people like being asked to help others, and this is one of the reasons why this simple visualisation can be so powerful.

What you have also done is change your perspective. You have permitted your right brain to create a vivid movie of a positive outcome in the future. Furthermore you have also changed your perspective by being the observer, and watching yourself behave with unconscious excellence in this movie.

Whenever you consciously change your perspective you always profit from this new viewpoint. Apart from anything else you will see yourself with greater clarity, and more accurately as others see you. The alternative is to continue living in a self-deluded world. It may appear to be a more comfortable world, but will always be more restricted.

Sometimes there is a danger that future goals can feel very remote, and may even discourage you from starting your journey. However, when projects are broken down into small steps suddenly the most impossible task seems much more reachable.

Float Like A Butterfly. Sting Like A Bee

Not surprisingly most if not all great athletes, and not just golfers, have incredible visualisation skills. Their imaginations are so creative that they may be a little embarrassed about describing their visualisations to others.

Muhammad Ali was perhaps the greatest boxer of all time, and developed powerful visualisation skills. One of my colleagues met him, and asked for the secret of his success. He sighed wearily, and explained again for the thousandth time,

'I float like a butterfly and sting like a bee.'

My friend understood the 'sting' but was still confused by the 'butterfly' metaphor. Muhammad Ali leant closer and whispered,

'I imagine floating out of my body like a butterfly.'

He imagined that he was standing at each corner of the ring and watching the fight from above. When he saw a muscle ripple in the shoulder of his opponent he knew what type of punch was coming his way, and had more time to take avoiding action. Now that is what I call visualisation.

Albert Einstein had magical visualisations too. He explained that that most of his creative thoughts were in pictures, and that he rarely thought in words at all. This is proof that a picture, or visualisation, is worth more than a thousand words.

Another powerful visualisation if you have difficulty finding the right swing tempo and rhythm is to picture your favourite golfer. Imagine you are watching him or her on the practice ground for a major tournament, and study their swing.

Then walk over to the slot next to your favourite golfer and start hitting a few balls as well. Try to use the same tempo and rhythm, and when you have done this follow Ali's example. Float out of your body and merge into your favourite golfer's body and imagine what it feels like to be that person. Enjoy hitting a few balls too. The more powerful your imagination, the more revealing and interesting your insights will be.

Using Visualisation To Develop Self-fulfilling Prophecies

Life is a journey of discovery, and learning more about yourself, about golf, and indeed about the rest of your life is not as difficult as it might sound. There is a time when the left brain is switched off for several hours, and this is when you sleep and dream.

For it is during this time that the deeper structures of your brain are working the hardest. It is when the events of the previous day are analysed and catalogued and it is when remaining problems are examined from every angle, and it is often when breakthroughs occur.

I know many people who keep a pencil and a piece of paper by the side of the bed, and when they wake up at three in the morning with the answer to a problem that has puzzled them for a long time they write it down lest they forget it.

I'm not suggesting that you should do this, but I do suggest you give your unconscious mind a mission to tackle while you sleep and dream. A little direction is a good thing because otherwise the brain will start thinking its own thoughts, and these might not be so helpful.

Your brain is an incredibly powerful computer. Some people claim that every experience is remembered and never forgotten. Whether that is true or not it is certainly true that our brains remember millions of events that have occurred over the years.

For example, your brain can remember many of the golf shot you have ever played. It can differentiate between the good shots and the not so good shots, and it can work out where the good shots came from. So think of your bad shots in a different way – think of them as great learning opportunities.

Suppose that you are faced with an important decision or problem – it could be about golf, or something completely different. Just before you drift off to sleep say to yourself, 'As I sleep and as I dream I will examine this situation from every possible perspective, and enjoy finding the best answer for the authentic me.'

When you wake up do not be surprised if the problem feels less important or urgent. You may not have found a solution, but you will feel as if you have made a great start.

We can also quieten the busy activity of our left brain and allow deeper thoughts to surface by learning to meditate. Meditation is, like hypnosis, an altered state with an inward focus of attention on a few stimuli, and not as complicated as it sounds. The more you practice meditation the more successful you will be.

You will develop a tranquillity where no particular situation has any greater significance than any other – where there is little difference in the way that you view good fortune or misfortune – knowing that there will always be great successes to more than balance the misfortunes that are part of life, and that by remaining calm is the best way to guarantee this.

In the next chapter you will discover how it might be possible to use Universal Energy to make your life a lot easier. This would include your golf too.

Meditation Booth

Three Nuggets For Now
1.

2.

3.

CHAPTER 9.
UNIVERSAL ENERGY – HOW TO USE EXTERNAL ASSISTANCE – AND NOT BE DISQUALIFIED

Exploring The Out Of Bounds

Universal Energy is the title of this chapter, and I will attempt to explore the boundaries of what we know[1], (believe firmly in the truth or certainty of something) and what we believe[1] (accept that something is true or real).

These should be two distinct subjects, although the definitions are very similar. The boundaries between these definitions are even more blurred. It is the murky world of the known unknowns, and the unknown unknowns. We do not get much clarification from modern philosophers either. Bertrand Russell concluded that all our knowledge ultimately rests on and is built up from instinctive beliefs[12].

This is therefore a world in which I step cautiously. It is a world very alien to my objective training as a doctor, scientist, and MBA. It is also a world that fascinates me, and so I am prepared to explore it a little further

What is it that enables ordinary men and women to perform the most extraordinary deeds? Tiger Woods and Phil Mickelson are ordinary people. Run them through an MRI scanner, and their anatomy is very similar to yours. The young men I talk to on the European Tour are very ordinary. Only when a golf club is in their hand does the magic flow.

When I think of such things Tiger Woods is always in there somewhere. I researched his scoring record in the fourteen Majors that he has won up to January 2013. I discovered some statistics that appear to defy the law of averages. Not for the first time I concluded that Tiger creates his own laws.

Many people have told me that Tiger wins Majors because he closes out in the final round better than anyone else. This perception is not the reality. The truth is that the final round has never been his best round of the tournament and on five occasions has been the worst round of his tournament. He scores what is necessary to win, but not much more.

Contrast this with his scores in the second round. On six occasions this was his best tournament round, and on every occasion he scored under 70. This is when his opponents were put to the sword.

What does this mean? I am not sure, but my instinct tells me that it is important.

Law Of Attraction

The law of attraction instructs us that positive people attract other positive people to them. This is not too surprising. We all know people we like to be with, either at work or in our personal life.

We also know many people who we do not choose to be around. Such people are the habitual moaners, and see the worst in any given situation. They are the energy vampires, and best avoided. They attract their own circle of like-minded negative thinkers. In extreme cases their energy can be destructive, focussing on negative emotions such as paranoia, jealousy, and anger.

The law of attraction not only postulates that positive people attract other positive people to them, but also that positive events attract further positive events. The law goes even further, and proposes that positive thoughts can lead directly to positive events, even at considerable distances. If even a fraction of this statement is to be believed then the implications are immense.

Its devotees use their own models to describe the law of attraction, but the consistent message is that energy follows our thoughts. In some way this energy expands to influence the event that was the focus of our original intention.

Many grounded and pragmatic people who have never even heard of the law of attraction, let alone put it into practice, nevertheless believe some strange force is out there, working in their favour. The words they use include luck, coincidence, synchronicity, serendipity, fate, and karma. They explain that a particular event was meant to be, or that things just fell into place.

French surgeon Alexis Carrel won the Nobel Prize for Medicine in 1912. His techniques for rejoining blood vessels are still used in transplant surgery to this day. Surgery is by necessity a practical specialty, but Carrel was a controversial free thinker too. He also believed that unseen forces can shape our destiny.

'Intuition comes very close to clairvoyance; it appears to be the extrasensory perception of reality.'

These ideas are not original, and similar theories were proposed by Napoleon Hill in his book Think and Grow Rich. This book was published in 1937, and is still a best-seller, with over 60 million copies sold, so at least it worked for Hill. Many of its readers were convinced it worked for them too.

Curiously, some people seem to be lucky at whatever they do. We can all think of examples of people who we know that sail through life with apparent serenity.

Paul McKenna believes we create our own luck. He writes[19],

'Whether you choose to believe in the law of attraction or not, it's interesting to note that many highly successful people do.'

The Product Description for his book Change Your Life In 7 Days highlights the same message.

'Success and happiness are not accidents that happen to some people and not to others.'

I believe this too. I cannot prove it, but I have seen enough examples in my own life and the clients that I have worked with to convince me. So how can you use the law of attraction? If the film and book The Secret is to be believed it is a lot easier than you might expect.

The Secret instructs us that all we have to do is 'Ask, Believe, and Receive', and let the power of the universe take care of everything else. For some people this is enough information, and they are probably already following this or a similar mantra. Others will doubtless require more convincing. What possible explanation can be given to them? If there is an answer it is hidden deep within the unconscious mind.

Scientists now broadly accept the huge influence and power of the unconscious mind, and yet their research has not even begun to uncover the tip of this iceberg, indeed not even the uppermost ice crystal. On the one hand this is frustrating, but on the other it means that your opinion is just about as valid as anybody else's. Perhaps the law of attraction is yet another example of the unseen power of the unconscious mind.

Asking is no more than the vivid visualisation of our list of skilfully constructed objectives. We have already considered the power of visualisation, and how Nicklaus used this for his golf. Others might prefer to describe visualisation as a list as affirmations, or more simply as a wish list. To the unconscious mind the distinction between reality and perception is blurred, to say the least.

Critically the difference between successful people and the majority is that successful people have created an intricately detailed representation of what they want, using all their five senses. This visualisation is so convincing that part of their mind believes this success has been achieved already.

Other parts of their mind fuel this overarching goal. They construct repeated rehearsals of the milestone events that will ultimately lead to this success. Putting this strategy into practice enables successful people to examine a forthcoming job interview or sales pitch from every conceivable angle. They develop exhaustive 'What if..?' scenarios.

As a result they are rarely taken by surprise, approach such important events with grounded confidence, and often walk away with a lot more than they bargained for. We can do the same. The fastest path to success is to follow what works for others. Not only does this include embracing their strategies, but equally importantly it involves binning the self-limiting beliefs that we and others have skilfully installed into our minds over the years.

Believing is just that. Believing takes a leap of faith, and requires an open mind. Most of us have been persuaded over the years into believing that success comes only from hard graft. That practice makes perfect. If something sounds too good to be true, then it is too good to be true.

All of these statements are true most of the time, but they are not always true. How is it that some people float through life with a smile on their face, are very successful, and make it all look so easy?

It is because they are good at asking, and they are able to believe with total conviction in their eventual success.

Receiving is also a tricky concept to explain. Sometimes it is easier to give a gift to another than to receive one yourself. The law of attraction requests that we watch for signs, that we interpret the events around us within the context of what we have asked for. That reception is an active process, and not a passive one. Receiving is not waiting for the universe to tap you on the shoulder with a wonderful gift. The gift is already out there waiting for you; you just have to find it.

One thing is for sure, we all miss a huge amount of vital information that is right in front of our faces. Information that could change our lives. More accurately we do not miss it, we just do not recognise it for what it is. These signals are processed literally just behind our face, but often with critical errors.

Our mind takes multiple huge shortcuts, and largely sees what it expects to see, based on previous experiences. That is why it is so difficult to see a hologram for the first time. The image is there, and processed accurately by the visual pathway. Yet it is rejected by the higher brain centres because it does not fit the expected pattern.

When we see, hear, or feel something so unusual that it is rejected by our conscious mind the echo of this memory still persists in our unconscious mind. It causes a feeling of uneasiness, similar to the irritation of an unfinished conversation, until it finds the right environment to surface. This is intuition, and like any other skill can be improved with practice. Poet and author Robert Graves knew its value.

'Intuition is the supra-logic that cuts out all the routine processes of thought and leaps straight from the problem to the answer.'

The lesson here is clear. Open your mind to as many sensory signals as you can, and search for any clue relevant to your desire. The only way you can do this is by putting all your attention in the present, and this takes much practice. Resist the pressure to be dragged back into a blinkered view of the world that has been conditioned and reinforced by previous failed outcomes.

Be prepared to experiment with different options. It is not likely that success will arise from repeating previous unsuccessful efforts. Indeed Einstein defined insanity as doing the same thing repeatedly, and expecting different results.

Trust your intuition and instincts, but always ask yourself, 'What is the risk?' This is the safety net, because while instincts are often proven to be correct, there are occasions when they can be spectacularly misplaced, with dire consequences.

Whether you can accept the possibility that the law of attraction can work for you, or maybe not, why not try it and see? Living life with a positive attitude has got to be a lot more fun than expecting everything to go wrong. This is sometimes described as the half full bottle mind set, as opposed to the half empty bottle.

So at the very least these ideas merit further reflection, irrespective of their current debatable scientific basis. The law of attraction has contributed to the happiness of many of their supporters, and can do the same for you too.

Is there a contradiction here? Surely the law of attraction is about thinking of the future, and what we want? Yet we have already considered the importance of staying in the present. How can both arguments be valid?

A possible explanation is that the law of attraction considers the future to have already happened. You have made your wish, and there is little more that you can do to fulfil this wish apart from stay in the present, do the best job you can, and wait. What will be will be. This is a perfect introduction to the law of surrender.

Law Of Surrender

There is another universal law that is also the subject of contentious debate. It is called the law of surrender. This law is also known in golf as 'Letting go', and somewhat irreverently by one of my clients as 'So what?'

Dan Millman describes what he calls the law of surrender in his book, The Laws of Spirit – A Tale of Transformation[20].

'Surrender means accepting this moment, this body, and this life with open arms. Surrender involves getting out of our own way and living in accord with a higher will, expressed as the wisdom of the heart.'

At first sight this does not appear to have much to do with golf, but on further reflection perhaps it has everything to do with golf.

By now you may fully understand that the secret to great golf is getting out of the way, and letting your body take over naturally. In other words disconnecting the logical and analytical left brain, and reconnecting the creative and playful right brain.

A recurring theme in my work with golfers is their restless yearning to play like a child again, with innocent self-belief[9]. Children are naturally 'right brain.' As they grow older they adopt 'left brain' behaviour, with the encouragement of supposedly wiser adults. Sadly this does not often help their golf, nor does it help many other things too.

The battle between the conflicting agendas of left and right brain summarises why so many golfers become increasingly frustrated, why their game suffers, and why this vicious circle continues. It explains why they want to return to the child golfer.

It also explains why hard practice, lessons, DVDs, books, and all manner of other training aids can help, but they are sometimes of limited and temporary benefit only. One way to break this circle permanently is to adopt those parts of the law of surrender that resonate deep within you. Walter Hagen expected to make 7 bad shots per round, and so will you too, irrespective of your ability. Accept it, and do not waste your energy fighting it.

Millman writes,

'Although The Law of Surrender means accepting whatever happens in your life, it does not mean passive toleration for what you don't like, or ignoring injustice, or allowing yourself to be victimised or controlled. True surrender is active, positive, assertive — a creative commitment to make use of your situation, in a spirit of appreciation.'

In other words, acceptance is not an excuse for scoring poorly, but more of an opportunity to triumph over adversity. When golfers work this out, they move to a much higher level of golfing awareness. They describe the physical and mental relief of 'letting go.'

Sometimes this awakening arises from personal tragedy, and subsequent achievements may become a legacy to a loved one. Very often golfers are able to reach hidden heights of ability when they play unselfishly for others, rather than for themselves. This is a possible explanation of Colin Montgomerie's superb Ryder Cup record.

A poignant example of leaving a legacy for a loved one concerns Steve Webster. He won the Portugal Masters in 2007 with the European Tour's best winning final round of the season, a 64 in Vilamoura. Webster's only previous European Tour victory in over a decade as a pro was the Italian Open[21].

'I lost my mum in the early part of the season and it really knocked me about..... It was so hard out there, coming down the stretch. I was thinking about my mum all the time and it was hard to keep my mind on the golf. But I know she was watching out for me today and I know she'd be proud.'

When I describe the law of surrender to clients I always have a nagging discomfort with the words. Words are incredibly powerful forces for good, or not so good. That is why the First Rule of Quantum Golf is so named. If the words are wrong the other two rules will not have a leg to stand on.

My disquiet concerns surrender. The word conjures up images of defeat and waving white flags, of the towel being thrown into the boxing ring. I have struggled for months with the word surrender. I always ask clients for their opinions, and ask them if they can think of a better alternative. I particularly liked the earlier suggestion, the law of so what?

Law Of Permission

Again writing as the doing part of thinking came to my aid. Whilst preparing material for this book the word permission leapt out of my unconscious mind. It was the missing part of the jigsaw that I had been searching for.

So was the law of permission born. Ordinary people do ordinary things. However, ordinary people are also capable of extraordinary feats of achievement. Most ordinary people sense this; the feeling they are capable of more, that more is out there, but they do not know where to look. Perhaps that is the enduring attraction of The Secret, and the many other best-selling self-development books that cram the bookshops.

Ordinary people, or at least some of them, require permission to think big, and to believe that the impossible is often the untried. From an early age we were told not to stand out from the crowd, to be modest, and self-effacing.

There are good reasons for this. As already mentioned, arrogance in others is not attractive. The Juniors were especially unhappy at the risk of being judged arrogant. On the other hand underachievement is too high a price to pay for modesty too. Each one of us will have our own ideas where to draw the line, how to balance these conflicting issues.

This is where permission fits in. What feels uncomfortable to you can feel very different when another person reassures you it is OK to believe that you are capable of more. When another person confirms that there are some things in your life that you can do better than others it somehow feels more acceptable. It is all right to know that you have a gift that few others have. More accurately, you have a gift you share with others. The difference is that you know it, and they do not. So make use of it. This is another example of how your brain responds more positively to another person's voice than its own.

Many of the better golfers I work with carry labels such as dyslexia, attention deficit disorder, or autism. Curiously, they often score very highly on the Right Brain Quiz too.

I instinctively distrust these labels, but do not wish to be too simplistic or dismissive of them either. My concern is that too easily these labels can become self-limiting beliefs, and powerful negative post hypnotic suggestions.

What is often forgotten is that there are positive qualities that go with these labels, but these are rarely highlighted. For example many dyslexics score highly on visualisation tests[22], and this might explain why, in my sample at least, they tend to be amongst the most talented golfers. It might also help to explain the genius of 2012 Masters champion Bubba Watson, who is convinced that he has attention deficit disorder.

The excellent book Seeing Spells Achieving describes visualisation exercises in detail, and would be doubly helpful for any golfer with dyslexic tendencies.

One of my clients is a talented young player. He was the clear leader with 3 holes to go in an important 36 hole competition. It was the most important competition he had ever played in. His thoughts drifted to winning, and then making the winner's speech. He had done a great job of staying in the present until then.

Within seconds his feelings had metamorphosed from a warm positive glow to utter panic. The wrong videos were playing in his head. Public speaking was his nightmare. Memories of dyslexia at school, reading the lesson in Assembly, and being humiliated by teachers came flooding back.

He double bogeyed the last three holes, and came second. That is why I do not like labels.

So if it helps I give you permission to think big. I give you permission to recognise that you have unique gifts. At the same time I remind you that in every other way you are an ordinary person. I hope this is reassuring. It means that you can remain humble and grounded too, and your friends will still like you.

One thing is for sure. Golfers with huge visions win Majors.

Embracing the law of permission could be one of the greatest steps you can take on the journey of life. One of the benefits is the recognition that progress comes from practicing smarter, and not harder. Another benefit is being able to play with the innocent self-belief of a child again, shooting your best scores, and experiencing the simplicity of living in the present.

Skier Julia Mancuso also adopted the law of surrender with brilliant results. She wrote after her unexpected Olympic gold medal win in 2006.

'I thought all I had to do was ski fast to the bottom. I wouldn't make it any more complicated than that ...

Sometimes that's all it takes. Sometimes, everything takes care of itself.....'

Indeed it does. In the next chapter I will venture into the even murkier world of quantum physics in an attempt to further identify the magic ingredient, and how it can work for you.

Meditation Booth

Three Nuggets For Now
1.

2.

3.

CHAPTER 10.
MIND OVER MATTER – HOW TO CONTROL YOURSELF, YOUR GOLF, AND YOUR RESULTS

Staying In The Present

I receive many, many emails from clients around the world, asking how they can deal with distractions on the golf course.

There will always be distractions. You cannot change distractions, but you can change the way you think about them. A long list of distractions would include weather, wind, cameras, aircraft, birds, spectators, playing partners, shadows, leaderboards, and mobile phones.

Stephen Hawking was advised by his publisher that every equation he used in his book would lose him 25% of his readers. I am hoping that golfers are a more forgiving breed, because I really like this equation that Karl Morris uses.

$P = p - i$, where P = performance, p = your potential, and i = the results of interferences.

Even I can understand this equation, but the conclusions and how you can use them for your golf do require a little more thought. You have some choices, and every client has their preference. Do you prefer to increase your potential through options such as practice, diet, exercise, coaching, new clubs, and mind control?

Or do you prefer to minimise the results of distractions through more effective mind control? Whichever choice my clients make I make sure we deal with both. It is noteworthy that mind control is the only example that applies equally to both options too, and should therefore be the biggest bang for your buck.

Almost all top players have mind coaches, and recognise the critical role they have played in their success. It surprises me that it is still often necessary to remind players that mind coaching is not for those who lack mental strength; it is for those who have already proven their resilience in golf, or in any other area of their life. Successful people are not afraid to discover just how much higher they can climb. Those who ignore the importance of mind coaching are unlikely to reach their potential, which is a great shame. We can all think of examples of players who were more than good enough to win a Major, but never did.

The law of surrender is one of the keys to deal with distractions. Expect these distractions to occur, and you have started to accept them. Striking out at them like a coiled snake will not help you or your golf.

I see this at first hand when I work with players on the Tour. Understandably a few of the players hope for a cathedral type atmosphere of calm reverence. Whilst this would be ideal they can consider themselves lucky if they get it. It is easier to expect distractions and deal with them as they arise, as they surely will.

I remember an amusing conversation with an Australian caddie in Aviemore over a beer. He was complaining that his player had been particularly difficult that day, and was inventing ever more ingenious distractions. His caddie finally told him to 'man up' or he was quitting. I had never heard that expression before, but there are times when it can be useful. I am not sure what they say on the Ladies tour, but they are certain to have a similar expression.

Almost all the work I do with clients can be summed up by the words staying in the present. Finding as many ways as possible to switch off the left brain and all its worries and negativity.

Another variant of questions relating to staying in the present concerns the Curse of the Winning Card. I suspect we have all at some time fallen victim to this ancient curse.

The Curse Of The Winning Card
Knowing you have a great card in your hand can be the Kiss of Death – The Curse of the Winning Card.

Another danger of knowing you have a great score is succumbing to the temptation to protect it. It is not just club golfers who succumb to the curse either. Webb Simpson's caddie ordered him not to look at any leaderboard during the final day of the 2012 US Open. Harrington's and Westwood's caddies have also issued similar instructions to their players at key moments.

This is how the curse spreads its infection. You have put yourself into contention by playing magical Right Brain golf. You are right in the zone. There is no faster way to lose the zone than by allowing your logical and analytical Left Brain to take over, and then the self-sabotage asserts its insidious influence.

Thoughts such as,

'Golf is not supposed to be an easy game. It must be time to hit a bad shot, just when I've got a real chance of winning now, so let's play safe.'

Or even the usually disastrous thought,

'Let me try something different, and see if this works!'

A tour client has identified mid-round technical corrections as always disastrous, but still finds them difficult to resist. Does this sound familiar?

Staying in the present is critical to performing well in any area of life. Generally people spend too long worrying about events from the past that continue to drag them back. They similarly spend hours worrying about events in the future that may or not happen.

The same is true of golf. If you allow your mind to flutter like a butterfly backwards and forwards it does not allow any room for concentration in the present. Worse still the past memories we dredge up are usually negative, of missed putts, pulled drives, and so the list continues. These memories develop a life of their own and catapult forward to thoughts of future outcomes. The usual result is a self-fulfilling prophecy of failure in the present.

Fortunately, there are ways to overcome it. The more you practice ignoring your card the easier it becomes.

Similarly the more often you put yourself into contention the more skilfully you handle these situations.

On occasions I present seminars with PGA Head Professional Roly Hitchcock. Roly has developed a unique skill in ignoring his score. His brain has found a way to work out his score unconsciously, transmit the message to his hand, write the score on his card, and then forget it. I have yet to discover how exactly he has done this, but will not quit until I find out.

Until you have reached Roly's level here are some tips that have helped some of my clients stay in the present. You do not need to remember them all. Just trust your unconscious mind to choose and remember the ones that feel most appropriate for you.

• Don't think of results – only process, and having fun.

• Do not add your score as you go along, nor check scores after nine holes. Golf is an eighteen hole game.

• Ignore comments from others about your great score.

• Quiet the mind with simple mantra – the more you meditate the easier this will become.

• Stop thinking. If this is difficult then recite nursery rhymes, count the trees, only think about golf when you are in your pre-shot routine. One client shot his best ever score whilst reciting Baa Baa Black Sheep for 5 hours. This is a comment, not a recommendation.

• Imagine you are surrounded by a cocoon of blue light, like being in a bubble, or in the zone.

• Focus on a distant point for 10 seconds whilst waiting for your partner to play. Do not move a muscle, or even blink for 10 seconds. Wearing dark glasses may help.

• Defocus your eyes as you walk, and concentrate on slow easy breathing.

• Take a lucky token with you.

• Concentrate on counting how many different sounds you can hear, how many different birds you can spot, how many horizons (layers) you can see, how many feelings you recognise, for example the breeze on your skin, the feel of the grass under your feet, and your breath entering and leaving your mouth and nose.

- Think of a time when you were happy, confident, and athletic.
- Recite the 17 x table.
- Listen to another voice in your head.
- Develop a rock solid pre-shot routine that excludes all other thoughts, and make it your 40 second sanctuary.
- Perhaps you might like to put a red spot on your glove!

As a Certified HeartMath® Sports Professional I am increasingly convinced of the vital role that breathing techniques play. I use them myself every day, and with all my clients. They proved particularly successful during the 2011 Scottish Open, as described in the conclusion. This is an extract from Science of the Heart,

'For centuries, the heart has been considered the source of emotion, courage and wisdom. At the Institute of HeartMath (IHM) Research Center, we are exploring the physiological mechanisms by which the heart communicates with the brain, thereby influencing information processing, perceptions, emotions and health. We are asking questions such as: Why do people experience the feeling or sensation of love and other positive emotional states in the area of the heart and what are the physiological ramifications of these emotions? How do stress and different emotional states affect the autonomic nervous system, the hormonal and immune systems, the heart and brain?.......

.... The answers to many of our original questions now provide a scientific basis to explain how and why the heart affects mental clarity, creativity, emotional balance and personal effectiveness. Our research and that of others indicate that the heart is far more than a simple pump. The heart is, in fact, a highly complex, self-organized information processing center with its own functional "brain" that communicates with and influences the cranial brain via the nervous system, hormonal system and other pathways. These influences profoundly affect brain function and most of the body's major organs, and ultimately determine the quality of life.'

Heartmath have a wonderful website, and much of their information is free. It is well worth a visit.

Discrepancy Events

Sometimes our valiant efforts to stay in the present are insufficient to overcome the pent up emotions surrounding our duel with golf. When all else fails think of something as vivid, surreal, and out of context as possible. This gives a Taser-like shot to the brain, so squeezing out most thoughts associated with golf. This is called a discrepancy event.

I could give examples that tour players have used successfully, but on this occasion prefer you to use your own imagination.

Quantum Physics

The world of science might have something to offer too. You will be the judge, so here goes.

A golf hole is made of nothing. There is nothing too surprising in that statement.

According to quantum physics, a golf ball is also made of almost completely nothing, and so too is a golfer. The majority of what appears to be a golf ball or appears to be a golfer is really just empty space, surrounded by a small amount of matter.

Almost everything in the universe is nothing. If you could extract all the matter from our population it would just about cover your ball marker. Everything else is nothing, just empty space between the smallest subatomic particles. It is rather like staring up into the sky on a clear night, where the stars are the equivalent of our subatomic particles. The rest is empty space.

This space in one sense though is not empty. Energy travels through it. This energy includes gravitational effects from stars. It also includes radio waves, and radiation, and all the other components of the electromagnetic spectrum. The only part of the spectrum you perceive is the tiny bit you can see – the visible light.

The two greatest breakthroughs in physics during the last century were the advances in the theories of relativity and quantum mechanics. Leading physicist Stephen Hawking writes in A Briefer History of Time [23],

'Today scientists describe the universe, in terms of two basic partial theories, the general theory of relativity and quantum mechanics.'

Relativity concerns very large objects and quantum theory very small ones. A quantum is the smallest discrete quantity of a physical property such as electromagnetic radiation or angular momentum[1].

Quantum physics is the study of energy and matter, and their complex relationships. Many eminent scientists were and continue to be excited by quantum theory. Not least because quantum theory opened considerable debate about actual reality and perceived reality, and the blurry area in between. In the last chapter we discovered just how blurry this area is.

So what does this have to do with golf? Perhaps it has nothing to do with golf at all, or perhaps it just might. Rightly or wrongly quantum theory has been used to explain the blurry area between our perception of reality, and where the power of the mind could produce an effect on matter. It is also the area where both ancient and modern philosophies meet science head on.

Some top athletes openly talk of the benefits that their thinking around quantum theory has brought to their game. Rugby Union star Jonny Wilkinson described a breakthrough in his fight against his fear of not achieving his goals when reading about the quantum thought experiment, known as Schrödinger's Cat[24].

'The experiment was conceived by the Austrian physicist Erwin Schrödinger to demonstrate a conundrum at the heart of quantum physics: that a subatomic particle exists in two states. However, the act of measuring it effectively forces it into one particular state, rather as England's discounted second-half try in the 2007 World Cup Final appeared to many fans to be both a try and not a try, until the referee called for a video replay.

Schrödinger sought to illustrate the strangeness of this phenomenon by imagining a cat in a sealed box with a jar of cyanide and a piece of radioactive material. There is a 50 per cent chance, at a given time, that the material has decayed to trigger the release of the poison. At that time, quantum physics says, the cat is both alive and dead.

As soon as one opens the box, the cat is either alive or dead, however. Observing it has made it so.'

"It had a huge effect on me," Wilkinson said. "The idea that an observer can change the world just by looking at it, the idea that the mind and reality are somehow interconnected . . . it hit me like a steam train."

Not surprisingly, this blurry area has also attracted more than its share of controversy. At its extreme interpretation any event that is unexplainable can be attributed to quantum physics in action. This is very convenient, because such a statement cannot be proved to be false.

It is not only just athletes who subscribe to the benefits that quantum theory promises. So too do at least some of the scientists who coach and study them. Mayer-Kress stated in his keynote conference presentation[25],

'Since quantum computation seems to be a macroscopic reality, it would be very surprising if natural evolution would not have developed means to exploit this computational resource that could give our biological brains - running more than a million times slower than today's notebook computers - the impressive computational capabilities that we observe in today's athletes. In terms of physical processes it is also clear that the microscopic events that lead to a decision to activate (or not activate) certain muscles during a movement process are fundamentally of a quantum nature, namely the electro-chemical processes in nerve membranes.'

Could this be a possible explanation of how advanced visualisation techniques enhance performance?

A further example of how quantum theory and its link to sport are gaining traction is the following extract from an article written by Guardian columnist Dara O Briain[26],

'There are those who think the arid world of this most obtuse science has little to do with football, believing the beautiful game can mainly be explained away through a combination of ballistics and psychology. They are ignoring the very cutting edge of the field.

In quantum mechanics, much is made of the moment where all the potential outcomes of something, the location of a photon of light, say, must reduce down to just one when a measurement is made. Until the measurement occurs, goes the theory, every possible solution is valid. You may have heard this mentioned in the dilemma about Schrödinger's cat. It's in a box and maybe it's dead or maybe it's not dead: we just don't know until we open the box and look in......

... This is high-powered stuff for physicists. It is, however, everyday talk for the average football fan.'

Although this was a light-hearted article it generated considerable comment. It provided proof that at least some readers found this subject thought-provoking. Quantum physics is by far the most complex subject I have ever researched. The only reason that I include it in a book about golf, albeit with considerable trepidation, is that it is a subject of increasingly common debate. It just might explain how some people seem able to control their lives more skilfully, and achieve more success, than others. If so, perhaps quantum physics forms the magical energy behind the law of attraction.

Hawking too shared Einstein's belief that a new theory will one day unify the theories of relativity and quantum physics. He calls this a quantum theory of gravity.

Unfortunately such a theory would present an unprecedented challenge[23].

'Yet if there really were a complete unified theory, it would also determine our actions – so the theory itself would determine the outcome of our search for it.'

It does not seem as if an answer to these questions is likely to surface soon. However, Jonny Wilkinson has found these ideas helpful, as have others. I keep an open mind, and am prepared to entertain any belief that causes no harm. Others are less open, and may ultimately be proven right. However, my reservation with a wholly dismissive approach is that we might just be missing something very important.

Whether you choose to subscribe to quantum theory or not, few would argue that if you use the same gifts that work in your life on the golf course too, and ditch the dogma, your golf is likely to improve. Swim with the current of the universal laws – go with the flow.

In an earlier chapter I mentioned that top golfers are physically very similar to you. Using a computer analogy their hardware includes bone, muscle, and brain just like yours. However their software system is very different. It is great for playing golf, but it might not very good for some of the other things necessary for life. Padraig Harrington is a typical example, according to his wife, Caroline[27].

'Padraig and household chores do not go together. I've taken him to the supermarket with me perhaps twice and it was not worth my while. I don't think he knows how to write a cheque and he doesn't know that our cheques have his name on the bottom of them. But he is very good at routines.'

Returning to the electromagnetic spectrum, perhaps the greatest athletes can tap into energy in ways that are beyond us. As a top coach suggested to me, perhaps special people like Tiger just have longer aerials than the rest of us, and so pick up more signal. Then they can unconsciously see or use a wider band of the electromagnetic spectrum than is available to us.

If this is so, then this metaphorical or metaphysical aerial must be rooted somewhere in our right brain. Other top golfers too seem able to produce the most amazing shots when they are most needed.

The best recent example concerns Phil Mickelson's third round in the 2010 Masters, specifically holes 13, 14, and 15. As Mickelson stood on the 13th tee he was in the chasing pack at one under par for the day.

As he walked off the 15th green he was six under par, having narrowly missed a putt that would have given him three successive eagles. I lost count of the number of times that the normally phlegmatic BBC commentator Peter Alliss used the word 'magical.'

It looked as if Phil was going to win again in 2012, when he coasted round the back nine in just 30 shots during the third round. It was only one virtually unplayable lie during the final round that cost him the tournament.

Einstein believed that such events that seemingly defy the laws of probability will one day be explained[28].

'Einstein thinks he has a continuous field theory that avoids 'spooky action at a distance', but the calculation difficulties are very great. He is quite convinced that someday a theory that does not depend on probabilities will be found.'

I'll finish with an interesting little snippet that I saw in the Metro in 2010. It concerns the successful collision of two subatomic particles at the speed of light in the Large Hadron Collider.

'There are known unknowns out there, like dark matter and new dimensions about which we hope to learn', said Cern research director Sergio Bertolucci. 'But it is possible we will find some unknown unknowns which could be hugely important for mankind.'

I found these comments rather frightening. My fears increased during 2011 when scientists discovered that neutrinos travel faster than the speed of light, which is impossible if the law of relativity is to be believed. Worse was to come a few months later when the scientists checked their calculations again and found they had put the decimal point in the wrong place, or something. These are the same people who collide subatomic particles at the speed of light relying on unknown unknowns. By comparison golfers are the most sensible people on the planet.

So how might quantum energy help your golf, and what are your options? Start with an open mind. Then inwardly reflect on your thoughts. Remember the times you did find the zone, and try to remember how you got there. Devote a little more of your life to living in the right brain, because this is where you are most likely to find quantum energy, if it does exist. You will also find the zone there.

Meditation Booth

Three Nuggets For Now
1.

2.

3.

CHAPTER 11.
CONCLUSION – IS THAT IT, THEN?

Well, I guess it is. I have pushed much information in your direction, deliberately so. I know that you will absorb much of this unconsciously, so there is little if any risk of overload.

I also know that clients process this information in different ways. Some slowly digest almost everything, while others just find one or two nuggets that resonate deep within them, and take off. These are the clients who skip at least one of the levels on their golfing journey.

Neither has any advantage in the long term. Or putting it another way, both are equally good, as we all end up at the same place. The only difference is the journey to reach the destination.

In my work with clients there is often one moment of breathtaking clarity that propels them forward from whatever their issue was. Frustratingly neither client nor coach can predict when this moment will occur. It could be within the first minute of the consultation, or surface as if from thin air a year later. A common expression that therapists use is,

'All at the rate and speed that is appropriate for the individual.'

It sounds trite, but it is true.

You probably have at least two questions going round your mind right now. If so, they are probably,

'Do these methods work?'

'Can these methods work for me?'

These methods do work, and have been tested at the top level. Clients have won Europro events, and graduated to Challenge Tour successfully. They have used them on the European Tour with success too.

During June and July 2011 I worked with Greig Hutcheon, and we enjoyed some great times together. Greig posted some impressive scores too. Our first event was the Wales Open, where rounds of 72 - 72 - 68 - 74 earned 28th place.

In the Scottish Challenge rounds of 67 - 72 - 65 (low round of the day) - 75 earned 22nd place.

From my perspective Greig's finest performance was in the Scottish Open. The tournament was cut to three rounds, and in a world class field scores of 68 - 72 - 68 earned him 49th place.

Scorecards provide the numbers, but do not tell the story. The 2011 Scottish Open went down in history as the 100 year storm. There were two landslides, flooding almost everywhere, closed car parks, and several spectators slipped and broke bones. The course was all but unplayable. So why was this Greig's finest hour?

The first day was showery, the rain took the sting out of the greens, and scoring was low. Watch out in future if the fairways and greens are firm. Castle Stewart will be a tough course.

Greig started the second round from the 10th tee at 13.40 in light rain. By the time he reached the 15th tee the sky was almost black over the estuary, and we could see lightning a few miles away. It was only a matter of time before play was suspended, and the hooters sounded at about 16.00, leaving Greig an eight foot birdie putt on 18 to look forward to. To cut a very long story short Greig completed the second round at about 22.00 on the third day, almost 32 hours later, and after multiple play suspensions. He also missed the putt. He had too long to look at it.

This round was the ultimate test of Greig's concentration, and my role as a coach too. Not only did he have to contend with the play suspensions, the foul weather, but also the luck of the draw. The early starters on the second day avoided the carnage. As the second round had already started there were no preferred lies for the late starters. Most of the time Greig's ball was covered in thick mud, and his round of 72 would have been worth at least 65 in kinder conditions.

During this 32 hour marathon round of golf Greig executed the Heartmath breathing techniques we had prepared, and I am sure they were instrumental in helping him to stay in the present.

We worked together again in August at the Johnny Walker in Gleneagles, but Greig was carrying injuries and missed the cut. This was a disappointment for both of us, but carried an unexpected bonus, not for Greig, but for me. I returned home early and was stiff after a long car drive. I needed to stretch my limbs with some gentle exercise and decided to play nine holes at my home club, and scored a hole-in-one on the 3rd. Was this quantum physics at work again? Greig was not amused, as he is still waiting impatiently to join this exclusive club.

Almost a year later I have other clients on the main tours, and hope to report their successes too. The tour circus is a strange life, and a common phrase is 'I just need one good week.' It is true. There are not many jobs where this is the weekly mantra, and where your life can be transformed overnight. I hear myself saying the same words too. Then I remind myself to focus on the process, and allow the results to take care of themselves.

So this is a long answer to the short question of 'Do these methods work?' I could have detailed many other stories, but this one is special to me.

'Can these methods work for me?'

They certainly can, because they have worked for so many other people. If they can work for them, then so too can they work for you. However it will take some effort and commitment, but probably less than you think.

Writing is definitely the doing part of thinking, and I hope you did make some brief notes. I recommend you collect them all, and put them on one piece of paper. Look at them often, and ask yourself the questions, 'How can I use this today? What shall I do differently? What is my plan? What are my objectives, and where do I want to be a year from now?'

We have explored some complex issues together, albeit sometimes at a superficial level. On the one hand it is very difficult to explain the commonalities that connect the strands of Zen Meditation, metaphysical philosophies, NLP techniques, hypnosis, body awareness, quantum physics, and universal laws to a central philosophy of golfing success.

On the other hand it is difficult to ignore the truth that great thinkers throughout history agree, even if they use different models, on the overarching intrinsic interrelationship of mind, body, and soul. When these elements coexist in perfect harmony ordinary mortals are capable of superhuman performance, even if only fleetingly.

It would take a lifetime of study to understand a fraction of some of the subjects that I have presented. One thing that I hope I have contributed is that whilst these subjects are separate, they are also loosely intertwined strands from the same rope. This is very important and I hope also reassuring for you. It means that you do not need to study each strand if you do not wish. Just select those that appeal to you the most.

This means that some of the benefits to your golf are in the bank already. You can be certain of one thing. Use these techniques skilfully and your motivation, confidence, and golf scores will take care of themselves.

Whatever Next?

I trust that you have enjoyed reading this book about golf. I cordially invite you to become an online member. It is free, and all I ask from you is your name and email address. My web site address is http://www.drstephensimpson.com and you have my promise that your details will only be used by me, and never divulged to anybody else.

In return you have access to various coaching resources, and my monthly newsletter. I welcome your contributions, and every month there are enticing free or other special offers.

Write to me with your comments, and questions. I reply personally to every note. I do this with pleasure and appreciation. Client feedback is the single most valuable commodity I have. Without it I have no way of calibrating my methods. Nor can I gain further understanding of what goes on in the largely unexplored area between a golfer's ears.

One question still remains stubbornly unanswered, and may have to wait for my next book, or even longer.

'Is golf a sport, obsession, compulsion, or addiction?'

Thank you for sharing this journey with me.

Meditation Booth

Three Nuggets For Now
1.

2.

3.

References

1. Encarta World English Dictionary (2009). Developed for Microsoft by Bloomsbury Publishing Plc.

2. The Times (December 22 2009). Phelps going to great lengths still in search of the impossible.

3. Rotella, B. (2008). Your 15th Club. London, UK. Simon & Schuster

4. Gallwey, T (1986). The Inner Game of Golf. London, UK. Pan Macmillan

5. Taylor, J (2009). My Stroke of Insight. London, UK. Hodder Paperbacks

6. Bradley, N (2005). The 7 Laws of the Golf Swing. New York, USA. DK Publishing

7. O'Connor, J & Seymour, J (2002). Introducing NLP. London, UK. HarperCollins Publishers

8. Jenkins, S (2009). Annual Review of Golf Coaching. Sport Psychology, Hypnosis and Golf, 149-172. Brentwood, UK. Multi-Science Publishing

9. Simpson, S (2008). Annual Review of Golf Coaching. Sport Psychology, Hypnosis and Golf: A Commentary 179-183. Brentwood, UK. Multi-Science Publishing

10. Jenkins, S (2008). Annual Review of Golf Coaching. Zen Buddhism, Sport Psychology an Golf, 215-236. Brentwood, UK. Multi-Science Publishing

11. The Times (June 14 2010). With a win in the US now under my belt, mind games could lead to more glory.

12. Warburton, N (2010). Philosophy: The Classics. Abingdon, UK. Routledge

13. Csikszentmihalyi, M (2008). Flow. New York, USA. Harper Perennial Modern Classics

14. The Independent (June 20, 2010). Psychology of sport: how a red dot swung it for Open champion

15. Nicklaus, J (2005). Golf My Way. New York, USA. Paperbacks

16. Jenkins, S. (2005). Sports Science Handbook: The Essential Guide to Kinesiology, Sport and Exercise

Science. Vol. 2. Brentwood, UK: Multi-Science Publishing Co., Ltd

17. Byrne, R (2006). The Secret. London, UK. Simon & Schuster

18. Hill, N (2008). Think and Grow Rich. London, UK. Wilder Publications

19. McKenna, P (2004). Change Your Life In 7 Days. London, UK. Bantam Press

20. Millman, D (1995). The Laws of Spirit – A Tale of Transformation. Novato, CA, USA. H J Kramer/New World Library

21. The Times (October 22 2007). Steve Webster's second win moves him to tears.

22. Bendefy, A & Hickmott, O (2006). Seeing Spells Achieving. London, UK. MX Publishing

23. Hawking, S (2008). A Briefer History of Time. London, UK. Bantam Press

24. The Times (September 19 2008). Quantum physics puts new spin on Jonny Wilkinson's life.

25. Mayer-Kress, G (2001). Complex Systems as Fundamental Theory of Sports Coaching? Keynote presentation to the 2001 International Sports Coaching Symposium of the Chinese Taipei University Sports Federation, Taichung, Taiwan

26. The Guardian (April 10 2010). What would Schrödinger's cat have to say about Rafael's sending-off?

27. The Times (January 19 2009). Padraig Harrington, the mind-games champion

28. Einstein, A (1971). The Born-Einstein Letters. London, UK.

Printed in Great Britain
by Amazon.co.uk, Ltd.,
Marston Gate.